Family Walks and Hikes
of Vancouver Island

Volume 2

Family Walks and Hikes of Vancouver Island

Volume 2
Nanaimo North to Strathcona Park

THEO DOMBROWSKI

RMB

RMB | Rocky Mountain Books Ltd.
rmbooks.com
@rmbooks
facebook.com/rmbooks

Cataloguing data available from Library and Archives Canada
ISBN 9781771602815 (paperback)
ISBN 9781771602822 (electronic)

All photographs are by Theo Dombrowski unless otherwise noted.

Cover photos: Squirrel on tree © iStock.com/Morlaya, Family walking a trail through lush green forest © iStock.com/mikespics

Printed and bound in Canada by Friesens

Distributed in Canada by Heritage Group Distribution and in the U.S. by Publishers Group West

For information on purchasing bulk quantities of this book, or to obtain media excerpts or invite the author to speak at an event, please visit rmbooks.com and select the "Contact Us" tab.

We acknowledge the financial support of the Government of Canada through the Canada Book Fund and the Canada Council for the Arts, and of the province of British Columbia through the British Columbia Arts Council and the Book Publishing Tax Credit.

Disclaimer

The actions described in this book may be considered inherently dangerous activities. Individuals undertake these activities at their own risk. The information put forth in this guide has been collected from a variety of sources and is not guaranteed to be completely accurate or reliable. Many conditions and some information may change owing to weather and numerous other factors beyond the control of the author and publisher. Individuals or groups must determine the risks, use their own judgment and take full responsibility for their actions. Do not depend on any information found in this book for your own personal safety. Your safety depends on your own good judgment based on your skills, education and experience.

It is up to the users of this guidebook to acquire the necessary skills for safe experiences and to exercise caution in potentially hazardous areas. The author and publisher of this guide accept no responsibility for your actions or the results that occur from another's actions, choices or judgments. If you have any doubt as to your safety or your ability to attempt anything described in this guidebook, do not attempt it.

CONTENTS

AREA MAP

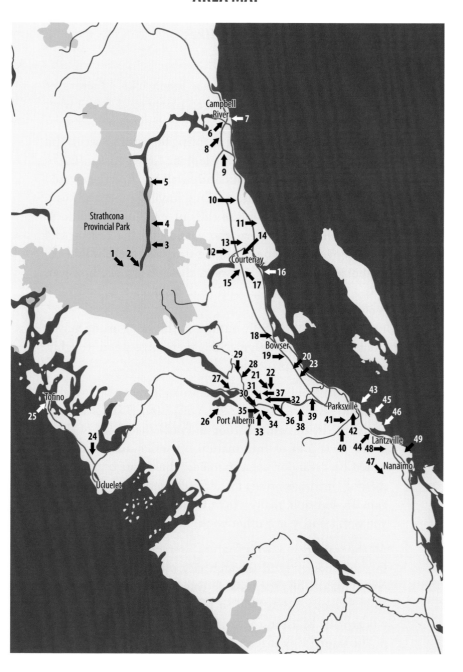

INTRODUCTION

Family Hikes

What makes a perfectly normal hike a "family hike"? There is, of course, no simple answer. We all have a pretty good idea of what doesn't belong in a book of family walks and hikes on Vancouver Island. A stroll through the beds of spring flowers in Beacon Hill Park is not what most families are looking for when wanting to take their brood for a dollop of nature walking. And they would blanch at the suggestion of assembling climbing ropes and heaving themselves *en famille* up the cliffs of 2200-m Mt. Elkhorn. No doubt, there are toddlers who would find the Beacon Hill Park option overwhelming and some strapping teens would call Mt. Elkhorn a jolly romp. Between these extremes, however, there is a rough middle ground that includes a considerable range of possibilities.

Unsurprisingly, the family outings in this book are as hugely varied as families themselves. Still, they correspond, roughly, to the following four principles:

1. Nothing in this book duplicates walks that can be found in *Seashore Walks of Vancouver* or *Popular Day Hikes of Vancouver Island*, by the same author and publisher. Both of those books have lots of information on walks and hikes that would be great for some families: these can be culled by reading the descriptions for difficulty, length and elevation gain. In addition, many of the trails described in this book you won't find in any other book.

2. All the trails here have a "natural" setting. Many fine walks in other books wind through city streets, along harbour fronts and so on. The trails in this book stick more or less to the woods. Admittedly, a few are surprisingly close to city streets: Millstone Creek Park in Nanaimo, for example, is surrounded by streets. It, however, and a few others

perilously close to city streets, are sufficiently large and full of ungroomed forest to create that sense of *Ahh* that comes with release from concrete and cars and the *Ooh* that comes with encountering huge old trees and gurgling streams.

3. Every trip in this book includes something special for children. Adults can be perfectly pleased walking sedately along a path that does nothing more than wind amongst second-growth forest. Children often have a hard time feeling such pleasure. They want an element of fun, surprise, thrill or the extraordinary. And who can blame them? Thus, each of the entries in this book comes accompanied by notes on what children might find interesting. The key word, of course, is "might." Nothing is less guaranteed in this world than a child's interest.

    Still, many children perk up when water hoves into view, especially if there is a chance – with or without parental approval – of interacting with the water. And the good news? A high proportion of the trails in this book link to streams, rivers or lakes. Of course, amongst watery delights, the mighty waterfall probably is the most fascinating. Not surprisingly, then, many of the trails in this book lead to waterfalls, some famous, some so obscure as to be known only by locals, but all of them impressive.

A word of warning: Many waterfalls can be viewed securely only from the top of a ravine. A good deal of parental judgment and care will necessarily go into assessing how much latitude to give the eager-beaver child who wants to go just…that…little…bit…farther.

On the other hand, most children are notoriously immune to the charm of The Pretty View. More good news: nearly all the trails in this book that lead up hills don't just provide a pretty view but also have something else – that airy King of the Castle excitement that comes from cliffy heights or (safe) rocky bluffs for clambering, or, of course, the perfect picnic spot.

Likewise, it's hard to pin down what will spark each individual child's interest in the natural world. What about huge, swarming ant hills, woodpecker trees, beaver lodges, spawning salmon, nesting herons or vulture updraft cliffs? You will find such features in the trail descriptions. The wily parent will use this information to whip up a little anticipation. The same wily parent can create anticipation about features that make viewing wildlife interesting – raised viewing platforms, suspended walkways, colourful interpretative signs.

No matter how fascinating nature walks are for some children, however, some simply don't like walking. Why walk, they wonder, when they can scoot about on two wheels? For such children (and, possibly, their parents), included in this book is information on which trails are suitable both for two feet and for bicycles (with, in most cases, sturdy tires).

Above all, and, indeed, in addition to all is that all-time highlight of any family expedition into the woods: the picnic! Although sandwiches and cookies can be devoured anywhere, knowing in advance about specific spots, and even picnic tables, can make planning a family outing huge fun.

4. No suitable parks have been omitted, but many of the trails are not in parks. It might seem unnecessary to direct parents to public parks which are, after all, public. This is especially the case with such high-profile parks as Mt. Douglas or Little Qualicum Falls. The fact is, however, knowing in advance exactly the best places to begin a walk, what facilities to expect, and, even more important, the trails within a park that are often overlooked can transform a ho-hum walk into a memorable family outing.

If the park you select is provincial, be a little more guarded than if it is national, regional district or municipal. While regional and municipal parks have increasingly shown impressive flurries of energy – new parks, new trails and new facilities popping up everywhere – sadly, the same is not true of provincial parks. Some are well served, of course, particularly if there is a popular cash-generating campsite associated with them. Many, however, are strikingly undeveloped or neglected. Broken boardwalks, faded signs, collapsed and eroded trails suggest that the provincial government has had different spending priorities.

Many of the best nature walks and hikes are mostly known only to locals. Look at the entries, for example, for Campbell River Beaver Lodge Forest Lands, Bear Creek Nature Park, Linley Valley – and you may realize that at least some of these have largely escaped your attention and your planning for a family outing.

Parks contain only a fraction of the trails on Vancouver Island. Outside of them, Vancouver Island is aswarm with trails – more trails than could fit into any book. Horse riders, walkers and mountain bikers have converted old deer trails, abandoned logging roads and just plain old wilderness into an astounding network of winding ways. Only a tiny selection of these trails is included in this book. These are the ones that, rather than just satisfy the interests of local users, also lead to a stunning viewpoint, pretty lake, rushing stream or lovely waterfall. In addition, this book includes trails that require little to no travel on gravel/logging roads: children are notoriously prone to car sickness on bumpy roads!

Because trails outside of parks depend on the enthusiasm of volunteers, you should still be prepared for comparatively rough conditions – but not always. Though wet spots are more common outside parks than in, volunteers have often built bridges and boardwalks or their loggy equivalent. Though bushes (especially salal) sometimes encroach, sometimes they are trimmed well back from the path. While signs are usually absent, sometimes they are inventive and charmingly placed just where they are most welcome. Flagging tape, rope on steep sections, stepping stones, banked trails and even benches sometimes show the enthusiasm of volunteers.

Usually all trail builders share each others' work cheer-fully. Sometimes, though, resentment can surface. Moun-tain bikers can be particularly susceptible to receiving such resentment, it seems, even though many trails that walkers adopt were originally carved out of the bushes by bikers. In fact, that is exactly the case with some of the trail descrip-tions here. A little gratitude, tolerance and cooperation can go a long way!

Erosion and mud holes result from heavy trail use. That, however, is the case no matter what the form of use. All trail use has an impact on nature. Specific conditions are sus-ceptible to different kinds of impact. Feet, tires and horse hoofs that can be invisible in some circumstances can create havoc in others.

Difficulty

While it is the common practice to designate a trail as simple, moderate or difficult, those terms are not helpful for families with toddlers and teens. What is easy for a teen may be insurmount-able for a toddler. In addition, the term "difficult" is itself unclear. A difficult trail may simply be long and tiring, or it may be short and steep, or it may have a section requiring sure-footedness and balance. So this book describes exactly what kind of difficulty you might encounter. The wise parent, therefore, will consider every-thing. Keeping in mind the ages, temperaments, interests and general physical fitness levels of the children, this wise parent will look at all three kinds of difficulty. A child who has decent endur-ance but is not sure-footed will be better suited to one kind of a trail than another. The reverse also is the case for a child who will happily leap across a log bridge and dart up a rocky bit of trail but is unlikely to last very long up a long, gentle climb.

When thinking about the length of a hike, you will find not here a whiff of information about the time to allow. When fac-toring in the toddler vs. teen, the dawdler vs. the eager beaver, the muddy track vs. the boardwalk, and then allowing for additional variations in distractions in the form of photo-ops, wildlife sightings, wading expeditions and so on, such information becomes meaningless. If you don't already have a good idea of the time to allow for your children to make it through X km of trail, then you soon will. Do remember, though, as you increase your planning skills, that each 120 m of uphill is – very roughly – equivalent to 1 km of horizontal walking. In addition, remember that while gradual downhills are at least as fast as horizontal paths, steep downhills can be slower than the uphill climbs, depending, again, on the sure-footedness of the child-trekker. The general advice, therefore? Always allow more time than you think you need!

Preparation

Once the trail has been chosen, next on the agenda is a little preparation.

Safety Issues

Safety, of course, is the single most important consideration. First, it is important to realize there is no such thing as a zero-risk walk or hike. There is no such thing as a zero-risk activity of any sort – including sitting in front of the television. On the other hand, there is little to no disadvantage in being a little over-prepared. Exactly what precautions to take will depend on many factors, amongst them your own temperament, the resilience of your family, the season and the remoteness of a trip.

Here, at least, are a few things to think about and take seriously.

Weather and Altitude

None of the trips in this book involves a great change in altitude, but don't be surprised if some of the hilltops are noticeably cooler than their bases. The usual advice about dressing in layers, including something waterproof, wearing tough shoes, bringing hats and sunglasses applies to the longer walks. If there is a single greatest danger, it is probably twisting an ankle in cold, wet weather at a remote location, such as Strathcona Park.

Though hypothermia is remotely possible, hyperthermia/heat stroke needs in some rare circumstances at least a little thinking about – but, of course, you've remembered the plentiful drinking water, sun hats and cool clothing!

Animals, Big and Small

Some trailheads are posted with warnings about bears and/or cougars, some of them indicating recent sightings. While, again, the risks of an aggressive encounter are tiny, they are not zero. Be sensible. In remote locations, it might be a good idea to keep small children close, to make a bit of a hubbub as you go and, possibly, carry pepper spray. Dogs can be a magnet for harassed bears and even lead bears back to their owners.

Tiny critters, like mosquitoes, can be a nuisance too, of course. You know the drill!

Wasps can be a significant threat, especially during picnics in late summer. Even when family members have no history of allergic response, the wise parent will carry an antihistamine like Benadryl just in case of a severe reaction.

Personal Health

Don't forget any medications that might be necessary, most likely for asthma or allergic reactions (in addition to insect stings). A basic first-aid kit is a good idea for all but the tamest walks. Children, as all parents know, can be highly inventive when it comes to ways of acquiring skinned knees – amongst other things.

Bits and Pieces

Backpack, binoculars, camera, walking poles.

* * *

You may well already be one step ahead in making these kinds of preparations. If not, you will soon be an expert. Now it's time to look at the weather forecast, pack the snacks, muster the troops and choose the perfect trail!

1. UPPER MYRA FALLS

A beautiful walk through Strathcona Provincial Park's old-growth forest to a viewing platform over the narrow, single shute of Upper Falls, which drops 60 m into a crystal pool.

LOCATION
Driving from Campbell River on Highway 48, go straight ahead onto Westmin Road when the highway to Gold River takes a sharp bend right to cross Buttle Lake. Drive to the end of Buttle Lake and all the way to – and right through – the Westmin wasteland of active operations 39 km along Westmin Road. As you leave the worst of the wreckage behind you, keep your eyes peeled for the signposted parking lot on your right where the road curves uphill.

DISTANCE
7.5-km round trip.

ELEVATION GAIN
70 m

DIFFICULTY
Generally easy, though fairly rough for small children in one section, and, of course, quite a long walk for stubby little legs.

SEASON
All season, though remember there may be some snow here even when the roads on the rest of the island are clear.

OF SPECIAL INTEREST FOR CHILDREN

The spectacle of the falls, shooting out of the forest opposite the viewing platform and dropping dizzyingly far below, has a high Wow factor.

1. Walk directly out of the parking lot and down the broad industrial road straight ahead. Particularly note the signs that read "Upper Myra," and the trailhead signed for 1 km ahead (actually a little less than that). Of special interest is the sign indicating that marmots (Vancouver Island marmots, unique to the island and a threatened species) have been reintroduced to the mountains ahead and are being monitored by helicopters.

2. Pass the Phillips Ridge trailhead and carry on until you see the small "Upper Myra Falls" post on your right and a misleading small trail leading up the bank. Passing a lovely patch of bunchberry, notice the venerable handmade sign for the falls posted high on a tree. Enjoy the many large, old-growth trees, principally hemlock and fir, in this section of virgin forest.

3. Most of the elevation gain is on the first part of the trail, though fairly gradual. The trail heads straight away from the trailhead before curving back and zigzagging up to a level height past devil's club and huckleberry bushes. From here the trail largely contours a heavily treed slope, dropping off to the left.

4. The next section of the trail passes through landscape churned up by recent avalanches and washouts. Although the way through is now clear, expect some fallen trees and large boulders. Older, moss-covered, giant chunks of fallen rock will remind you (and, with prompting, your children) of the dynamic forces of erosion on the mountain slope.

5. Come to a section of sturdily built boardwalk and hand-rail curving around and suspended over a steep section of

FROM LEFT Perspective from the viewing platform near the 60-m falls; one of the suspended walkways along a steep section of mountainside.

boulders. Immediately afterward, cross the sister bridge. You are now only 15 minutes from the falls.

6. A final section of suspended boardwalk brings you around a curve to a viewing platform for Upper Myra Falls. The narrow falls erupt from a slot in the forest directly across a chasm and drop into an emerald-green, crystal-clear pool.

7. Rhapsodize on your experience and return, buzzed, the way you came.

2. LOWER MYRA FALLS

Easy access to a spectacular series of falls dropping over giant steps towards Buttle Lake in Strathcona Park.

LOCATION
From the start of Westmin Road, as it leaves the Gold River Highway (28), drive about 35 km to the end of the lake. Rounding the end of the lake, the road starts to climb a hill. The large park sign for Lower Myra Falls is prominently positioned on the right. The large parking area reflects the popularity of this set of falls.

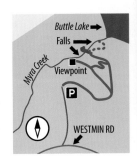

DISTANCE
1.4-km return (including the rough trail to the lowest part of falls)

ELEVATION GAIN
70 m (on return leg)

DIFFICULTY
The main park trail is easy, but the smaller, user-made trail to the bottom of the falls is a little rougher.

SEASON
All season, but remember that in winter Strathcona Park can have snow even when there is none at sea level. Even at the end of a dry summer, the falls put on a good show.

OF SPECIAL INTEREST FOR CHILDREN
The giant steps over which the falls drop are perfect for clambering, and some of the pools are suitable for (carefully supervised) splashing.

1. Leaving the parking lot, descend the broad, smooth trail until you get to the narrower trail leading to the left, signposted as "Upper View Point." Follow this trail to its end,

FROM LEFT Spray fills the air above the lowest falls, reached by a rough trail; Slightly down stream from the upper falls are many terraces of limestone.

overlooking the spectacular falls. From this point you can see the single largest drop, followed by a much shorter cascade, leading to a crystal-clear pool over slabs of flat rock.

2. Return from the viewpoint to continue downhill as the trail makes two large zigzags. When you reach a T junction, turn left to follow the trail out to the lower viewpoint. Because the falls have eroded a deep cleft into the rock, you will need to climb onto the flat areas of rock in the creek bed to get the best view of the whole sequence of falls above you. Be careful, especially with children, not to go too close to the edge in your attempts to see the falls below you.

3. From here, the established park trail leads back to the parking lot. However, for the best overall experience, take the narrow user-made trail leading into the trees and downhill to your left. This trail is a little rough but presents no real difficulties. It brings you to a shelf of rock only slightly above the lake and with a superb view of the lowest of the major falls as it drops into a small pool.

4. Return up this user-made trail. Turn left when you reach the main park trail to the lower viewpoint and follow the broad, gravelly slope back to your vehicle.

3. SHEPHERD CREEK

A loop trail in Strathcona Provincial Park, a section of which runs by a fast-running, crystal-clear creek and leads to a striking view of a deep emerald pool beneath a rugged cliff.

LOCATION
Turn onto Westmin Road at the Buttle Lake narrows. Drive 26 km to the Ralph River Campground. On the left side of the road is the sign for the trailhead.

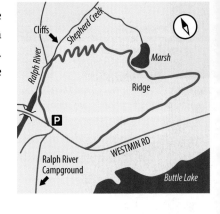

DISTANCE
1.5 km

ELEVATION GAIN
15 m

DIFFICULTY
Easy, but very small children might find the section of climbing a little tiring.

SEASON
All season, but be aware that snow may be present in Strathcona Park when there is none in Campbell River. Unlike some of the other creeks in the park, this one keeps an attractive level of water even at the end of a dry summer.

OF SPECIAL INTEREST FOR CHILDREN
While there is nothing especially for children, the very fact that the trail runs close to a burbling stream gives obvious opportunities for interaction! Nothing is more intriguing to most children than the water molecule.

1. From the parking lot follow the clear and well-maintained but fairly narrow trail past several large cedars and

FROM ABOVE Cliff and pool, upstream from last access point to the creek bank; Shepherd Creek near the confluence with Ralph River.

hemlocks. Before long you come to the banks of a creek. This spot is particularly interesting because from the height of the bank you get a good view of the confluence of the Ralph River and, closer, Shepherd Creek.

2. Although access to the creek itself is not easy here, the trail runs for a short distance close to and only slightly above the rocky, fast-flowing stream. Several large cedars bordering the trail lean picturesquely over the creek banks, exactly as they ought to. Shortly before the trail turns away from the bank, look upstream to an especially striking spot where a mossy cliff rises directly above a deep emerald pool. If this isn't a photo op, nothing is.

3. The trail turns away from the creek, bypasses some huge fallen logs and begins a series of about ten switchbacks (depending on how you count). The trail climbs up a slope bordering the end of a treed and mossy ridge, separating the trail from the now-distant highway.

4. As the trail levels out, notice the trees, mostly Douglas firs, are considerably smaller than they have been until this point. Through the trees to your left is a roughly circular, treeless, marshy area of reeds created by higher ground surrounding the slight depression.

5. The trail runs around the end of the marsh, making a broad sweep to the left. This section of the trail, with the marsh on the left and the ridge above you on the right, makes a striking contrast with the first part of the trail by the creek.

6. Once past the marsh, the trail rounds the end of the ridge and traverses its other slope. At this point, you are walking roughly parallel to Westmin Road and may hear the rush of occasional vehicles through the trees.

7. You may be a little disoriented when you discover that the trail comes out to Westmin Road a considerable distance from the entry trailhead. However, you should see your vehicle farther up the road, patiently waiting for you.

4. KARST CREEK

*Named because of the easily dissolved limestone ("karst")
rock that allows a little creek to sink underground and
reappear, but at least as interesting for a lovely set of falls
along the loop trail in Strathcona Provincial Park.*

LOCATION
From the junction with Westmin
Road and Highway 28 to Gold
River, drive about 17.3 km until
you see the carved sign for Karst
Creek.

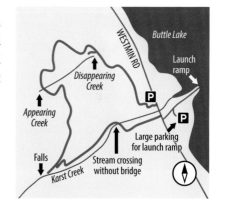

DISTANCE
1.8 km

ELEVATION GAIN
80 m

DIFFICULTY
Mostly easy, but since a bridge has been destroyed by flooding,
crossing the creek on stepping stones can be tricky if the water
level is high.

SEASON
All year, though in winter all Strathcona Park trails can have
snow even when there is none at the coast of the island.

OF SPECIAL INTEREST FOR CHILDREN
If there is enough water flowing, the disappearing creek and
reappearing creek can be good fun. Crossing the larger creek,
Karst Creek, by jumping from rock to rock can be a minor adventure. If you're up for a little edification, point out the burn marks
on the bark of the larger Douglas firs that survived a devastating
forest fire.

FROM LEFT The uppermost falls is best viewed by walking upstream a little from the end of the main trail; below the upper falls the trail continues downstream past many lovely cascades.

1. Begin at the signpost for the trail and climb gradually through an S curve until you come to a sign saying you have reached "Disappearing Creek." If you arrive in late summer when the water level is low, you might have to search through the sword ferns and young maples to find the tiny creek before you can see it disappearing into an eroded hole in the karst.

2. Zig up the increasingly rough and eroded path, ultimately crossing a little bit of boardwalk near the signposted "Appearing Creek" bubbling out of the ground. Note the lovely patch of maidenhair fern.

3. From this point the trail largely traverses around the slope until, rounding a corner and descending, you come to a view of Karst Creek itself. When you come to a fork in the trail near the creek, turn right, upstream. This is a dead-end bit of the trail, but it does take you closer to the pretty, little waterfall shooting out over a lip of rock.

4. Return to the junction and head downstream. The trail at this point descends a sequence of broad dirt and log stairs and passes an impressively engineered log bank stabilizer (at this writing, partially destroyed by flooding).

5. Because of the karst rock, the stream here can be largely, or even totally, under the streambed. The trail, however, leads down parallel to the creek bed a short distance and then crosses at the location of a former bridge (the concrete footings are still visible). If the stream is flowing briskly, however, crossing here can be anywhere between tricky and, at times, impossible.

6. From here to the trailhead the path is broad and smooth, descending gradually to Westmin Road. An easy walk takes you to the beginning of the trail and your car.

5. LUPIN FALLS

A short loop trail in Strathcona Provincial Park, making up in Wow factor what it lacks in length. The 40-m high waterfall is one of the highest easily accessible falls on the island

LOCATION
5.3 km south of Buttle Narrows Bridge.

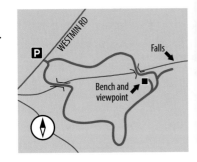

DISTANCE
1 km

ELEVATION GAIN
20 m

DIFFICULTY
Easy, with sturdy bridges (complete with guardrails), making stream crossing a pleasure.

SEASON
All season, but best in the wet season. Also remember that Strathcona Park trails, starting at about 400 m altitude, can have snow when there is none at sea level.

OF SPECIAL INTEREST FOR CHILDREN
Children will be doubtless as charmed as adults not just by the sheer height and beauty of this narrow waterfall but by the magical, grotto-like surroundings.

1. The trail begins in a flat area of large cedars and firs. Almost immediately you come to a substantial and artfully angled bridge crossing a stream – often dried out by the end of a dry summer.

2. After curving back to allow a good view up the stream (or, when dry, just a streambed), the trail begins to climb. Swinging

CLOCKWISE FROM TOP LEFT The view upstream towards the distant falls; Immediately across Westmin Road from the trailhead is a welcoming beach; the main falls is best viewed in a spring run off.

through a switchback, it traverses a ridge as the slope drops off increasingly steeply to the left.

3. Within minutes the trail levels out and begins to drop. Even from this point the lack of undergrowth and the mossy undulations amongst the widely spaced trees create an unusual atmosphere. This atmosphere deepens as the trail winds downhill past mossy boulders towards a railed viewing area and a park bench.

4. And the view! The knoll on which the park bench is perched looks directly across what Romantic poets might call a "dell" towards a rugged rock face and, startlingly high above, at about 40 m, a virtually vertical series of cascading drops – Lupin Falls. There is a minor thrill in approaching the base of the falls, but the best view is from the knoll.

5. When you finally tire of the splendid sight (possibly sustaining your troop with nutritional supplements), turn back to descend and cross the stream below the falls. Make your way back to your vehicle.

6. BEAVER POND/KINGFISHER TRAIL

One of many beaver-pond trails on Vancouver Island, combining a pond-side trail with a walk through large Douglas firs and hemlocks to the banks of the Quinsam River.

LOCATION
From the traffic lights at the northern exit of Campbell River, where Highway 19 intersects with Highway 28, drive 1.6 km towards Gold River. Immediately after crossing a small bridge over the Quinsam River, turn into a small parking area. Oddly, the trailhead is 300 m farther along the road, immediately opposite a concrete roadside barrier, but parking along the road there is difficult.

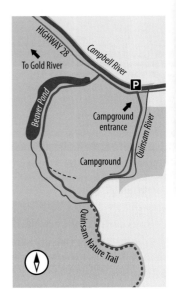

DISTANCE
2.9-km loop

ELEVATION GAIN
20 m

DIFFICULTY
Broad, smooth trail with some timber and dirt steps. Care needs to be taken crossing and walking along a short section of busy highway.

SEASON
All season

OF SPECIAL INTEREST FOR CHILDREN
Children will enjoy looking for spawning salmon in the autumn and for beavers (and kingfishers) during the warm months.

FROM LEFT Waterlilies and cattails at the south end of the beaver pond; the Quinsam River flows quietly near the campground.

1. Leaving your car in the parking lot used mostly by fishermen prowling the riverside trail, cross the highway, turn right and walk along the shoulder in the direction of Gold River. It is possible, alternatively, to walk along the riverside trail, but the point at which you should leave this trail to come back up to the highway isn't obvious.

2. Opposite a concrete barricade on your right is a yellow warning sign – but, oddly, no sign indicating you have reached the trailhead for Beaver Pond/Kingfisher Trail. The sign, also oddly, is a standard BC Parks sign usually used for backwoods travel, insisting, amongst other things, on self-reliance.

3. The trail, surfaced more or less with crushed gravel, passes ferns and alders, and heads straight away from the highway. After a few minutes you arrive at the marshy end of the long, narrow beaver pond. Except when the water is high, you might see little or no water. The fairly narrow but smooth

trail runs along the edge of the pond with a steep bank, covered with many bigleaf maples, rising up on your left.

4. Soon the trail ascends a fairly long sequence of timber and gravel steps. While traversing the forested bank, you see glimpses of the main part of the pond through hemlocks before beginning the descent, again over timber and gravel stairs.

5. Reaching the shores of the beaver pond, you see that it lives up to its name, both in looking like a proper pond and in allowing opportunity for a game of spot-the-beaver-lodge. Through the lacey boughs of hemlock, the pond, with its tussocks and water lilies, is particularly lovely.

6. The trail becomes wide and even as it angles away from the pond and climbs slightly. Although the forest is clearly second growth, the large trees, hung with moss and surrounded by sword ferns, do what they do best. When you come to a fork, ignore the trail to the left (a shortcut to the campground) and follow the trail ahead until, passing the campground on your left, you come to the shores of the Quinsam River.

7. In an ideal world, BC Parks would put a few resources into restoring Quinsam Nature Trail, which leads upstream to the right. At the time of writing, it is closed because of erosion at a few points, but a shift in spending priorities might mean the trail will soon be open again, allowing you a lovely walk up to the salmon enhancement site and back again.

8. Turn left to follow the shores of the river downstream. The bad news is that the rest of your walk back to your starting point has little wilderness feeling. The good news is that you can walk along the beautifully forested (largely fenced) banks of the river for some distance and cheerfully ignore the campground on your left. In addition, when you are forced onto the asphalt park road to return to the highway, you are still walking through attractive forest along a quiet, safe road.

7. MYRT THOMPSON TRAIL

A trail unlike any other on this part of the island, along the meadows and banks of the Campbell River as it passes through the estuary out to a lovely spit.

LOCATION
From the traffic lights at the junction of Highways 19 and 19A, north of downtown Campbell River, drive 800 m towards the centre of town. Turn left (towards the coast) onto Maple Street at a junction with a prominent Petro-Canada station. Drive the short distance to the end of Maple Street and park on the shoulder.

DISTANCE
2 km

ELEVATION GAIN
Negligible

DIFFICULTY
Easy, level trail.

SEASON
All season, though, of course, the character of the river, the type of birds displaying their plumage and vegetation change enormously with the time of year.

OF SPECIAL INTEREST FOR CHILDREN
Some parents will be able to womp up something close to fascination with the interpretative signs along the trail. Failing that, there are usually lots of easily spotted birds – great blue herons, eagles, Canada geese. Children who like to ride their bikes can (sedately) accompany their walking parents on bikes suitable for

The Campbell River is broad and gentle as it flows through the estuary.

gravel surfaces. Walking Butch, your (leashed) chihuahua, and picking blackberries are both possible here.

1. The narrow, but level and clear, gravel trail leads past a rubbish bin and under a grove of red alder to the grasslands and the colourfully carved Myrt Thompson Trail sign. If you've arrived exhausted, here too is the first of many benches dotting the trail.

2. Pause to ponder the wonders of nature provoked by an illustrated sign entitled "Return to the River." Although the trail is a little away from the banks of the river at first, there are many "windows" with picturesque views across the broad, slow river. At high tide, the shoreline itself is a little prettier (slimy rocks cooperatively out of sight) and the river looks more like a long, narrow lake.

The view upstream on the Campbell River.

3. Feel free to keep your eyes trained on the path and river rather than the abandoned asphalt lot on your right, particularly when you come to a bench allowing views upriver where two forks branch and where a few stately Douglas firs rise above the alders and maples.

4. The trail soon enters a particularly interesting phase as it runs along the narrow crest of a spit, with, on occasion, interesting old boats anchored on the right-hand side. Pause at two more interpretive signs.

5. At the end of the spit, cross an attractive wooden bridge to a tiny island. The trail ends, fittingly, at a suspended wooden viewing platform with a bench. With any luck you will be alone – with your picnic, your camera and/or your thoughts.

6. Return the way you came.

8. BEAVER LODGE FOREST LANDS

*A sequence of broad, level trails through large,
second-growth trees interlaced with small streams.*

LOCATION

If approaching Campbell River from the south on Highway 19, turn right onto Jubilee Parkway and drive about 1.7 km. Turn left onto South Dogwood Street and, after 5.4 km, left onto Merecroft Road. Drive just over 1 km, noting that Merecroft Road swings left and becomes Trask Road. Drive a short distance to the end of the road and park in the lot. A large sign of the whole area is posted here.

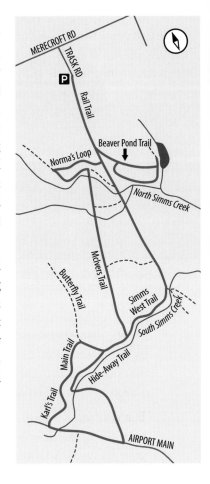

If approaching from Campbell River, you can drive uphill along almost any road until you reach Dogwood Street, the prominent thoroughfare running roughly north–south through the city. Once on Dogwood, turn left until you come to Merecroft Road.

DISTANCE

5 km

ELEVATION GAIN

30 m

DIFFICULTY

Easy, broad, smooth trail with barely any noticeable elevation gain.

SEASON

All season, but try to choose a sunny day when the light slants through the trees creating that distinctive "cathedral" effect.

OF SPECIAL INTEREST FOR CHILDREN

Although there is one small beaver pond that can provoke some interest, probably the chief attraction of this trail is for kids who like to zoom around on two wheels while their parents walk sedately or ride along with them. This is also one of the few trails where parents who know the route can be reasonably secure in allowing children to "run ahead to the next bridge."

Be aware: There are no fewer than five detailed maps of these trails online – and no two are the same! Although dozens of routes are possible, this combination of trails provides a good, substantial tromp, while generally keeping to the larger trees and more winding, woodsy trails.

---

1. Start out straight ahead on Rail Trail, a broad, level track that looks like a road. Within a very short distance, however, turn left onto Beaver Pond Trail to make a lovely little side loop. When this trail arrives at the pond in question, you might want to turn left at the T junction, simply to get some pretty views of the pond before returning to the same junction in order to go straight ahead to the other end of the pond. Once at the south end of the pond, via a narrow and somewhat bushy trail, swing right to make your way back to reconnect with the main Beaver Pond Trail and then back to Rail Trail.

2. Go straight ahead, crossing a large and uninspiringly functional-looking bridge. Once you have crossed two streams, still on this major thoroughfare, you come to South Simms Creek. Turn onto the signed Simms West Trail and drink in the sudden change to a comparatively small trail winding past some beautiful, big maples with tiny ferns sprouting out of leaning, moss-covered trunks. Don't expect too much

Beaver Pond is a photogenic conclusion to a small detour.

from Simms Creek itself – in the summer it is barely visible through the overhanging salmonberry bushes.

3. Ignore McIvers Trail on your right. Once you pass it, you notice your own trail becomes comparatively broad. Within a few metres of the junction with McIvers Trail, turn left onto Hide-Away Trail. This particularly pretty bit of trail winds towards and away from the creek. At the next junction, turn left to cross a lovely little bridge over South Simms Creek. After crossing another bit of creek, emerge from the forest and find yourself on a broad, charmless track.

4. Despair not. Turn right and follow this for a few minutes – yet again crossing South Simms Creek. Cross an ugly bridge and, immediately after, turn right onto Karl's Trail. Immediately after you see a sign on a tree saying "Simms West."

5. Pass by a small trail to the right. You are now on the unsign-posted Main Trail. When you come to a T junction with a

The bridge on Norma's Loop.

broad, smooth track lined with alders, turn right onto the south end of Butterfly Trail. Follow this trail, as you have before, until it narrows, and you come to another T junction. With the creek on your right, turn left to repeat a short section of the Simms Creek Trail. Soon come to signposted McIvers Trail, which you did not take on your outward trip. This time turn left and follow it straight ahead for a considerable way, ignoring two side trails on your right.

6. Arriving at another T junction, this one for Norma's Loop, turn left and very soon afterwards cross a lovely little bridge and turn right. Norma's Loop will bring you back out to Rail Trail on which you began your winding way, many, many twists and turns earlier. Turn left to arrive, very soon, back at your starting point.

9. WILLOW CREEK

Meandering trails through leafy forests over pretty bridges around a small, pebbly creek.

LOCATION

If you are driving north on Highway 19 towards Campbell River, watch for the sign to the Campbell River Airport, alerting you to the intersection you need. Don't turn towards the airport but right onto Jubilee Parkway. Go 1.7 km and turn left onto South Dogwood Street. After 350 m, turn right onto Erickson Road for 1.1 km. Turn right onto Martin Road.

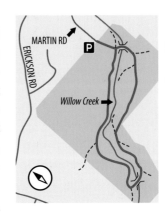

From Campbell River, it is easiest to drive south on Highway 19A, passing Oyster Bay. Look for a Shell gas station to alert you to Erickson Road. Turn right and drive 1.1 km until you see Martin Road on your left.

Park at the end of Martin Road in the turnaround area where you'll see a large sign and map for the trails.

DISTANCE
1.7-km loop, but seems longer because of all the twists and turns

ELEVATION GAIN
25 m

DIFFICULTY
Generally easy, but side trails can be bushy.

SEASON
All season. The creek remains pretty and flowing even throughout a dry summer, but by the end of the summer, the salmonberry bushes can be a little thick and obscure the view of the creek.

OF SPECIAL INTEREST FOR CHILDREN

This is the perfect beginners' trail – a lovely, safe, short loop for the littlest proto-hikers who want the independence of walking on their own. The creek bed itself is easily accessible just over halfway around the loop, and the bridges are great spots at which to drop in those tiny leaf or twig boats that then race their ways out of sight. Fall has additional possible treats because of work on the creek bed by Highway 19A; salmon have been observed making their way upstream if water levels are high enough.

1. Go straight ahead on the broad, level trail, under primarily alders and maples, ignoring the branch to the left. As you approach the creek, the trail swings a little left until you come to the clear area by the creek under fairly large cedars and hemlocks. An impressively substantial, raised bridge leads over the creek.

2. Once across the stream, ignore a branch to the left (leading out of the park) and other side trails to the right to keep above the bushy area down the bank to your right. Along this section you are primarily away from the creek, climbing noticeably, until you come to a series of steps.

3. Descending the steps, take the right option past two forks in a row until you come to the second large bridge crossing. Like the other bridge, this one is well above the creek, with lovely views of the bouldery, mossy creek bed and bushy banks.

4. Once across the bridge turn right (ignoring a fork to the left) to follow the creek back downstream. This first part of the downstream trail brings you close to the bank at several points. At one point, in particular, you come to an intriguing nurse log in the middle of the stream with a small hemlock clinging for dear life to it.

5. Although this first part of the downstream trail is fairly rough and bushy, once you come to a junction with a major

FROM LEFT The lower bridge across Willow Creek; an unusual little hemlock grows out of a nurse log in the middle of the creek.

trail (going out to Erickson Road), it improves dramatically. Cross one tiny bridge and complete the loop part of the trail by arriving back at the large trail near the first bridge. Turn left to make your way the short distance back to your vehicle.

10. BEAR CREEK NATURE PARK

Centred around a salmon enhancement project, this network of forested trails skirts the Oyster River and Bear Creek.

LOCATION

Driving north on Highway 19, part-way between Courtenay and Campbell River, watch for the large blue sign to Miracle Beach and turn towards it down Hamm Road. Just before you reach Highway 19A, turn left onto Macaulay Road.

Alternately, driving south from Campbell River on Highway 19A, look for Hamm Road on your right just after the signposted turnoff to Miracle Beach on your left. Almost immediately, turn right onto Macaulay Road.

Once you are on Macaulay, drive for just over 2 km and then watch for the attractively carved sign for Bear Creek Nature Park on your right. Drive down the gravel road about 300 m to a parking area. Here is a map of the whole park and beside it the gated gravel service road down which you begin your tromp.

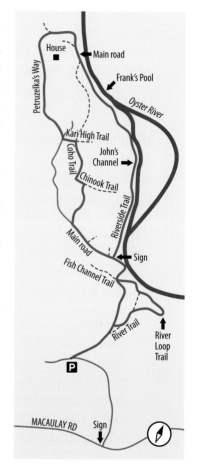

DISTANCE

2.8 km

ELEVATION GAIN

28 m

DIFFICULTY

The route is a combination of gravel service roads, broad tracks and narrow dirt trails interlaced with some rooty sections.

SEASON

All year. Oyster River (much more visible than the Bear Creek in the park's name) flows enthusiastically even throughout a dry summer. Fall is perhaps the most interesting as you can see the salmon spawn here (bolstered by a salmon enhancement project) in spawning channels where the salmon can be viewed at close proximity.

OF SPECIAL INTEREST FOR CHILDREN

Spawning salmon in the fall are the most obvious attraction, but the fast-flowing river itself is appealing. In addition, following the complex route through this maze of fairly short trails can be hyped as a bit of a treasure hunt. Cycling is permitted, and a stimulant for children who prefer a two-wheeled approach to path finding. Be aware the hill between the river flats and the parking lot is fairly challenging for little ones. In addition, there are a few spots on the side trails where the going is a little rough.

1. Begin by following the gravel service road (Main Road) downhill to the river flats where all the subsequent trails wander – sometimes a little dizzyingly. Cross a bridge and, shortly afterwards, come to a kind of crossroads. Turn right at the signpost onto broad, gravelled River Trail. The name is a little misleading because it dips by a small creek only briefly before bringing you to a junction with River Loop Trail.

2. Turning right onto River Loop Trail, find yourself passing through some amazingly mossed trees, trailing their fronds above the path. With the river occasionally visible through the maples and hemlocks on your right, carry on straight ahead, ignoring a trail on the left, until you emerge onto Main Road.

The Oyster River is a perfect spawning environment for the autumn salmon run.

3. Turn right and cross a bridge close to the river. After only a few metres on the road, come to a sign providing interesting information on the salmon spawning. Turn right onto Riverside Trail. Soon you come to a signpost (in the shape of a salmon, no less) directing you along John's Channel.

4. Some of the most attractive parts of the fast-rushing Oyster River are along this next bit of trail. The path becomes narrow and uneven as it curves away from the river to follow the shore of a spawning channel feeding into the river. Nearly dry in summer, the channel has some interestingly sculpted bits of sandstone.

5. Soon find yourself back by the main river flow. Take the time to walk down the little metal staircase to Frank's Pool and the little riverside grassy area with is park bench and standing rock sculptures.

6. Return to Main Road as it heads first along the course of the river then curves around the northern perimeter of the park and brings you to an open area with, surprisingly, a house.

A good place to pause before the route turns away from the Oyster River.

In fact, this is the club house of the good people who have worked on the salmon enhancement projects in the park. Walk past the fish-shaped sign for Petruzelka's Way to enjoy the colourfully presented interpretive sign at the Egg Take Station. Carry on down this broad track until you come to a trail on your left called Kari High Trail. As the name suggests, the trail was built by students from a local high school.

7. Go only a short distance on this trail until you come to a crossroads. Turn onto Coho Trail and go a short distance, until you come to a junction with an unsigned, pretty trail leading to your left (Chinook Trail). Turn left and, after a very few metres, turn right onto Cutthroat Trail to approach an interesting area of wetlands and fish incubation management.

8. Cutthroat Trail goes some distance, primarily under maples, merging with Main Road near the information sign you passed on your way upstream. Turn left to follow Main Road all the way back to your car. During spawning season, however, it is well worth your while to take a short wander up Fish Channel Trail, on your right shortly after crossing the bridge.

11. SEAL BAY REGIONAL NATURE PARK/ XWEE XWHYA LUQ

A long, easy loop trail, suitable for walking or bicycling, through mature second-growth forest. While a route on the seaside section of this large park is included in Seaside Walks of Vancouver Island, *this route circles through a different part of the large park.*

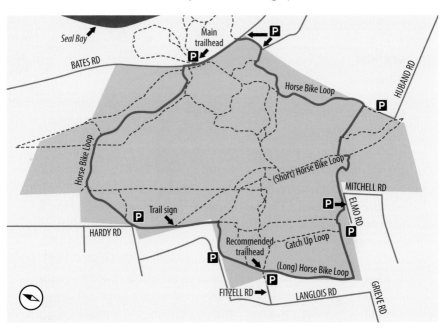

LOCATION

The main trailhead requires complicated navigation, so it is easiest to start at one of the minor trailheads a short distance off Highway 19A north of Courtenay. Measuring from the major intersection where Highway 19A leaves Cliffe Avenue and crosses the river, drive just under 6 km and turn right onto Grieve Road. Drive to the end of Grieve Road, about 800 m, then turn left onto Langlois Road, and, after another kilometre, right onto Fitzell Road. At the end of this short road is parking in the turnaround.

DISTANCE
10.75 km

ELEVATION GAIN
15 m, cumulative

DIFFICULTY
Easy, level track, much of it broad enough to allow two to walk abreast. Although there is a dizzying number of criss-crossing trails, signposts and maps make it easy to stay on Horse Bike Loop (described here).

SEASON
All season.

OF SPECIAL INTEREST FOR CHILDREN
This is a great place to come if you have children whose idea of a family outing is fun only if two wheels are involved. The tires should be sturdy enough to handle gravel and the occasional root. Signposts marking distance travelled give a motivating sense of progress. Strolling children will enjoy hunting for a menagerie of little plastic critters that have, apparently, taken up residence amidst the foliage.

1. Start down the broad track and turn right to join the main loop trail. A map is posted on a tree with a large red arrow indicating that, indeed, "You Are Here" at the Fitzell Road entrance. Note that three different versions of the map occur en route, not all of them with the same information. Notice the small sign indicating you are at the 5-km point of the loop: similar signs will help you track your progress. This part of the trail is one of the least inspiring of the loop because, essentially, you are following the property line of a farm.

2. Soon the trail takes a sharp turn left with a sign confirming that you are on the 10-km loop and pointing left. This next section of the forest is one of the most attractive, with its

blend of fairly large hemlock, cedar and fir. A small wet area has an interesting cluster of skunk cabbages.

3. Ignore the trail to the left to "Catch Up Loop" and, almost immediately afterwards, another trail to the left. Keep ahead past the 6.5-km sign; turn right to leave the forest and arrive at Elmo Road. Turn left.

4. After a short distance up Elmo Road where it meets Mitchell Road, turn left up a service road and pass a metal gate to a kind of service area. Look for a green and blue plasticized sign on a large fir that points straight ahead to the Horse Bike Loop. Here the trail makes a kind of S curve to the right but enters the forest again. Note that you need to turn right, then left, and then right again in fairly rapid succession. Fortunately, signs help you on your way.

5. A short distance ahead, pause at a particularly dramatic version of a nurse log. In this case it is not a log but a stump that is in the process of rapidly rotting and leaving the small hemlock clinging desperately to it and equally desperate in trying to send its roots into the solid earth so that, soon, when the stump is completely gone, it can still – just possibly – survive.

6. A sharp turn left at the next junction will start you on the northward side of the loop. When you come to a gate to block the way of horses onto a side route, there are signs pointing south to Huband Road, and another now indicating your forward loop as "Bike Route," heading forward to Bates Road.

7. Ignore a small trail to the left, following an arrow for the main trail, then, soon after, turn left to follow the 10-km sign indicating the main loop and delivering you onto Bates Road. Looking left down the road you should be able to spot a large parking area and the main trailhead for the seaside trails. Although following the main loop involves making your way down the road to this trailhead, directly across the road is a horseshoe sign on a tree indicating a trail, parallel to Bates Road, and leading towards the main trailhead.

FROM LEFT The otherwise complicated circuit is made simple through extensive use of signs; one of the strange tree formations in the park, this one a hemlock still surviving atop a rotting nurse log.

8. Opposite the large parking area is a fairly grand entrance to the network of trails (that don't lead to the sea). This is the network you want. Go about 10 m past this spot and turn left onto the trail. Amongst the many other signs is one for "Horse Bike Loop" and "Start of 7 and 10 Km Loop."

9. From here to your starting point, the route is largely straightforward. After a long uninterrupted stretch, pass three trails in a row leading to your right. When you arrive at the Hardy Road trailhead, cross the parking area, pass a yellow gate and an outhouse.

10. Along the last section of trail to your starting point, keep right at all intersections, even though at one of them is a sign merely saying "Trail" and pointing to the left, and no sign indicating your onward route. With any luck at all, arrive back at your starting point, a little tired but also elated.

12. UPPER BROWNS RIVER MEDICINE BOWLS

An easy walk along a broad, forested track to a riverbank with several steep trails leading to various rugged rock formations channelling gushing water through several drops and, in summer, through deep pools. The name I use here, "Browns River Medicine Bowls," like the alternate name, "Brown River Falls," is popular with locals, though neither is official.

LOCATION

From Highway 19 north of Courtenay, turn onto Piercy Road and drive to Forbidden Plateau Road about 1.5 km along. Turn right. After a few minutes, cross Highway 19 on an overpass. Start measuring. After about 6 km, when the road takes a sharp turn left, notice a rough gravel road going straight ahead. While it has been possible to drive down this potholed road, it has become so degraded that it is best to park at the beginning of the road and walk. In fact, the woodsy walk along this track makes a perfectly pleasant part of the outing.

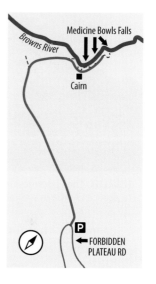

DISTANCE

3.6-km return

ELEVATION GAIN

100 m, cumulative

DIFFICULTY

As is the case with so many falls, the walk to the river gorge is easy. Thereafter? Not so much. The steep dirt-and-root paths descending to several spots along the sequence of falls are all potentially dangerous, especially if the trails are slick. The good news is that, when the water is high, it is possible to get a good

FROM LEFT The uppermost in a series of several cascades; the middle falls in winter, slowing to a graceful drop in summer.

sense of the power of the falls while remaining on good, if narrow, paths. Still, it's best to take only older and/or goat-nimble children – who will listen to their parents.

SEASON
In the summer, the medicine bowls are beautifully sculpted pools fed by small, vertical cascades. In the winter, the holes are lost in explosive torrents of narrowly channelled foam.

OF SPECIAL INTEREST FOR CHILDREN
With the proviso that the conditions are good and the children extremely careful and sure-footed, they can't help but be at least a little entranced by the falls.

1. The old roadbed heads gradually uphill more or less straight, through mostly firs and hemlocks. On the left you see a few bits of wreckage of a disintegrated mountain-biking trail.

2. When you come to a clearing and, possibly, a few parked 4x4s whose drivers braved the road and/or were unwilling to walk, the old road swings right. A short distance ahead is a split and the beginning of a much-trodden area of trails, all leading to the edge of the river, and views of the various sections of the falls. Prominent in the upper cleared area is a large brass and stone memorial cairn dedicated to two young men who were killed while swimming in the river. The message hardly needs to be spelled out.

3. The largest trail leads right and heads to the lowest entrance to the riverbed – and the large swimming hole. However, the last few metres of the trail are steep, and you cannot get a good view of the falls unless you go all the way down the trail. For the best secure viewing spots, therefore, it is best to seek out the smaller, upstream trails.

4. Return to your vehicle the way you came.

13. WILDWOOD TRAIL & ONE SPOT TRAIL

A locally built and managed trail through some beautiful, varied forest, with the option of riding bicycles.

LOCATION
From the Inland Highway (19), take the Piercy Road exit north of Courtenay, and drive for 2 km until you come to the power lines crossing the road. The signposted parking area for Wildwood Interpretive Forest is on your left.

DISTANCE
12.2-km part return, part loop (including a 4.6-km loop section)

ELEVATION GAIN
30 m, for the long version

DIFFICULTY
Easy, almost level.

SEASON
All season, except for the wettest weather.

OF SPECIAL INTEREST FOR CHILDREN
The chief attraction for children is that they can scoot on their sturdy-tired bicycles while their parents plod parentally along, or, of course, join their children on two wheels (in single file). There are also lairs of tiny, colourful dinosaurs, lizards and creepy crawlies that have escaped toy boxes and found homes in nooks and crannies of trees, especially along the Piercy Road end of the trail.

The trail surface generally makes for easy walking and mountain biking.

1. Within a few metres of the beginning of the trail, cross a small bridge and then come to a crossroads with Pipeline Trail. Pass through this small clearing with some huge cottonwoods to keep straight ahead on Wildwood Railgrade Trail. Ignore a trail to the left a few metres along.

2. Entering the stand of primarily Douglas fir and salal, keep ahead on the level dirt trail, ignoring the signposted Power Line Trail to the left. Turn left at a fork in the trail by two fairly large Douglas firs, when you see a sign high on a tree for Burns Road, and others for Wildwood Road and Piercy Road.

3. Pause at the signposted Cedar Tree to admire its girth. After a few minutes, at a bend in the trail, ignore the signposted trail to the left for Power Line Trail. Pass – or pause at – the bench. Arrive within minutes at Forest Hill Junction. Keep ahead on the Burns Road route, ignoring trails to Forest Hill and Power Line Trail.

4. You can relax and merely enjoy the gently winding, level trail for some time, until you notice the trees are suddenly much smaller. You have entered what is called a "plantation"

on some maps (planted in 1993), but, fortunately, you are out of it in a few minutes. Turn right, though the junction is not currently signposted. (If you want the short loop walk, turn left here and jump ahead to 8, below.)

5. Entering large second-growth again, you see a charming sign warning you that the next 400 m of trail is wet and slippery. This may have once been the case, but a new trail seems to have been built parallel to the old trail and, in most conditions at least, seems perfectly easy going – all the way to the Burns Road Trailhead.

6. Cross Burns Road and begin your exploration of Bob Webb Trail, significantly different in character from the trail so far. First pause to look at the beautifully prepared interpretative signs for Wildwood Interpretive Forest. Pass the yellow gate and go straight ahead along a dappled broad gravel track underneath young alders and firs.

7. When you get to a fork, look for a small sign with the image of a walking figure at the beginning of a carefully prepared trail leading right and slightly downhill. From here to the trailhead, the wide, gravelly trail winds through a broad S curve through fairly congested, small firs, before ending at a pleasant, meadowy, fenced spot with signs for Bob Webb Trail.

8. Retrace your route first back to Burns Road and then back as far as the plantation. Turn right at the fork to emerge from the plantation, passing by a bench, onto Gas/Hydro Service Road. Turn left.

9. This service road occasionally lives up to its name: it can be a little chewed up with service vehicles. Generally, though, it provides straight sailing under power lines through thickets of broom, before swinging slightly left and becoming a broad, grassy track going into the forest. Ignore all three trails leading to the left and proceed until you return to the trail junction near your starting point. Turning right brings you within a few metres of the Piercy Road trailhead.

FROM LEFT A typical section of forest with large, second-growth trees; a section of One Spot Trail, named after a historic locomotive.

Optional Add-On: One Spot Trail

For the ambitious, it is possible to add several kilometres of pleasant, flat riding or walking. Several features make the continuation attractive. First, the route, named after the historic "Old One Spot" locomotive, is dotted with many historically fascinating interpretative signs. Second, the route, level and flat, could hardly be more pleasant as a cycling or walking route (or for horse riding). Third, the route has a character unlike almost any other in this book – at points you might feel almost as if you've entered Ontario farmland, with light woods and meadows all around. Suggested here is a small section of the much longer One Spot Trail, but by far the prettiest because it lies farthest away from trafficked roads.

1. From the Wildwood Forest trailhead, cross onto the signposted One Spot Trail and go straight ahead to the split in the trail. By turning left onto the lane-like route you begin a 2.8-km section that takes you past meadows and farms to Fair Road.

2. At any point, turn back to retrace your route to the Piercy Road trailhead.

14. STOTAN/STOKUM FALLS & PUNTLEDGE/ BROWNS RIVERS CONFLUENCE

A short trail to a long, many-tiered falls with a swimming hole in summer, and, in winter, an ear-numbing and almost overwhelming impression of huge volumes of foaming water. The option of a much longer but easy walk to the confluence of the rushing Puntledge and Browns Rivers. Expect to encounter both names – Stotan and Stokum – and debate about the correct version!

LOCATION
From the Inland Island Highway (19), take the Piercy Road exit (#127) north of Courtenay. Drive 1.5 km and turn right onto Forbidden Plateau Road. After 800 m, turn left onto a broad, fairly smooth gravel road, Duncan Bay Main, and drive for just over 1.5 km, until you see a broad shoulder/rough parking area immediately before a significant bridge.

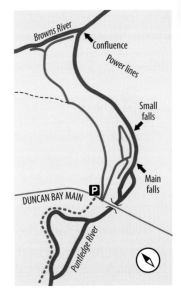

DISTANCE
1-km partial loop, partial return. Additional 2-km return on trail to confluence.

ELEVATION GAIN
10 m to Stotan Falls, 35 m to confluence

DIFFICULTY
Overall, an easy trail to the main falls, though a few logs have fallen over the narrow loop trail below the falls. There is a (minor) safety concern: because the flow of the river is controlled by a dam on Comox Lake, it is not impossible, particularly after a period of heavy rain, that a release of water could suddenly raise

Go in winter to view the falls at their thundering best.

the water level. A sign alerts you to the presence of a siren and warns you of the dire consequences should you ignore it. If you hear the siren, leave!

SEASON
Summer is the time to get wet and enjoy the deep green pools, but, for the jaw-dropping sense of power, the more water the better – and that means late fall through spring.

OF SPECIAL INTEREST FOR CHILDREN
Since this is one of the waterfall pools in the area that is most safely and easily reached, water-loving kids will make this one of those nag-the-parents destinations. The extended trail to the junction of the two rivers leads to a pretty beach, and, it goes without saying, a perfect picnic spot. It would be fairly easy for kids to ride bikes while parents walked to the confluence (not to the falls), but the hill on the return trip might involve a little dismounting and pushing.

1. Walk past the yellow flood warning sign on a clear trail. This trail takes you through an impressive bed of sword ferns

beneath maples. Within minutes, pass the crest of a first, fairly small set of falls clearly visible through the overhanging cedars.

2. Next visible through the trees is the striking view of a split in the river as it runs either side of a tree-covered island, swept by the increasingly rushing river. The level, broad trail will bring you within minutes to the descent to the river-bank, just downstream from this island. Although this path is a little awkward at spots, it is one of the easiest descents to a riverbank at any falls in the area.

3. After savouring the stepped falls, you can make a little exploration upstream on a small trail. Particularly when the river is full, this walk gives you more striking views of the river rushing past the rocky, treed island.

4. Next, make a loop walk downstream by heading first back up the path you used to drop to the river. Partway, turn right to the broad path running along the bank parallel to the river but considerably back from it. Within a short distance this path leads to a smaller track, dropping down to the right through waist-high sword ferns. As you approach the river again you have some good views of this part of the river with a comparatively small set of stepped falls, lovely in their own right. The path near the riverbank back upstream to the main falls requires some limber-limbed antics in climbing over a few fallen trees.

5. Complete the loop by joining the main falls trail halfway up the slope, turn right to climb the riverbank and return towards your vehicle.

Optional Add-On: The Browns/Puntledge Rivers Confluence

1. Returning to your vehicle, you see a very broad path – actual-ly, an old roadbed – near a sign on a tree showing a map of the land in this area donated for park land. Turn right down this broad trail. Follow it straight ahead through stands of maple and sword fern as it roughly follows the S curve of the

CLOCKWISE FROM ABOVE LEFT Puntledge River, near the confluence with Browns River; above the falls, the Puntledge River is still powerful; it is possible to get impressively close to the falls, even when they are full.

river. You are fairly high above the river, however, and far enough back in the trees that you get only the odd glimpse.

2. When you reach a distinct fork in the track, go right. The left track leads ultimately to fishing trails on the banks of the Browns River, and, after that, to some picturesque falls. Having taken the right fork, plough ahead down and up a distinct gully. As you rise to a crest you can see ahead down the significant slope through the broad swath of cleared forest under the power lines.

3. Go straight ahead on the broad trail through the broom thickets, ignoring a trail to the left. Upon entering the trees, find yourself within a very short distance of the wonderful jut of land with, on your right, a short trail to the rushing Puntledge River and, on your left, the smaller but equally vigorous Browns River. Clearly, it's time for a picnic. Come prepared!

4. On the way back from this unusual little spot, you may wish to take time to follow the trail to the right under the power lines, as it leads again to the shores of the Browns River. Any new river entry is interesting, but this one is only averagely interesting. Don't expect a thrill.

5. Return to your vehicle the way you came, trying not to register surprise at how much steeper the hill seems going up than it did coming down.

Optional Add-On: Nymph Falls

Upon reaching your vehicle, notice on the opposite side of the road a sign and a trailhead. This is the beginning of an old trail, originally a mountain-biking trail, along the shores of the Puntledge River, and ultimately leading to the park trails a short distance below Nymph Falls (described in Popular Day Hikes of Vancouver Island*). Without going the whole distance, you may wish to explore a little upstream. Amongst other things, notice the very different character of the gentle river here. Logs have collected in a major swarm at one curve, and the course of the river itself splits and joins again.*

15. PERSEVERANCE CREEK FALLS – MEDICINE BOWLS

Swirling, curving falls through smoothly sculpted deep pools and a creekside trail through magnificent cedar forest.

LOCATION

From the Inland Island Highway (19) take the Cumberland/Courtenay exit (#117). At the bottom of the exit ramp, turn toward Cumberland, just over 1 km away. Follow the main route along 4th Street into Cumberland and turn right onto Dunsmuir Avenue, the main street of the village. As you leave the shops behind

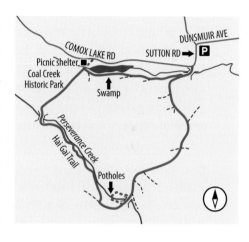

you, look for Sutton Road on the left. (Beware the road is called Egremont Road on the right.) Turn left into the large gravel parking area.

DISTANCE

5.4 km

ELEVATION GAIN

90 m, cumulative

DIFFICULTY

Overall moderate, but there are some sections on the creekside trail suitable only for sure-footed older children – or shepherded younger children. The optional descent from the view spots right to the potholes or medicine bowls (local names vary) is precipitous but easily avoided.

SEASON

All season, but the waterfalls are most spectacular during winter and spring. Locals like to flop into the lusciously cool bowls in summer when the water level is low – despite the difficult descent.

OF SPECIAL INTEREST FOR CHILDREN

The rushing creek has many exciting sections of rapids, logjams and, of course, the medicine bowls themselves – all of these most safely viewed from the trail. The route also passes through a section of historically interesting Chinese settlement from the coal-mining days. Old photographs and informative signs add a sense of mystery and bygone times.

Described here is the recommended loop route, starting on gravel road and concluding on a sequence of largely mountain-biking trails, part of a large network of trails around Cumberland. Many other routes are possible.

Beware: you can easily get disoriented. You can buy a colourful map of the trails in Cumberland's bike shops, but you may be dismayed to find the names of most trails appear only on the map. Few signs exist.

---

1. Leaving the parking lot, turn left along Sutton Road towards the clearly visible metal yellow gate at the end of the road. Walk past the gate and over a bridge to take the broad gravel road heading right and uphill. Follow this road as it climbs through a broad S curve. Many mountain-biking trails lead off on either side. Venture along them only if you are sure you won't get lost – and are ready to give right of way to cyclists. As you approach the high point, the trees open, allowing good views of the surrounded forested hills.

2. As the road descends, it brings you to a logging-truck bridge and good views down and up the rapidly rushing creek. You see small paths on both sides of the creek. While both of

these lead intrepid locals a short distance to the medicine bowls for summertime dips, the trail on the right as you face downstream is better. Not only is it more used but also it provides better views of the charging falls (in winter) or the deep emerald pools (in summer).

3. Return to the gravel road, turn right and continue for a few minutes until, on your right, you see a carved wooden sign: "Hai Gai" (a Chinese name with local historical interest). Be alert. The sign is a little distance down the trail and partly obscured by overhanging branches. This trail is actually a mountain-biking trail. Used as a descent, the trail was built as a technical route with steep ramps and log bridges. Many of these are broken down, so only a few intrepid riders are likely to pass by. Do be watchful, however, and be prepared to jump aside!

4. The trail alongside the creek is a real highlight of the route. After picking your way over some of the technical features – including a single-log bridge – find yourself close to the creek. Several minutes near the creek are followed by a gradual ascent as the trail traverses a slope and the trees thin out uphill. Along this section, the trail, though well-built and supported by small logs, traverses a steep bank above the creek some 30 m below.

5. Descending nearly to creek level, you soon pass a dramatic set of twisting rapids and a logjam. The trail rises again, and drops, taking you through some magnificent forest. Admire not just the large cedars but the yews – you are not likely to find such a concentration on many other easily accessed trails in the area.

6. A sign that tells you that you are entering Cumberland Community Forest indicates you have more or less completed your descent. In extremely wet weather you might have to hop across a small stream before passing an especially lovely grove of cedar and coming to a sturdy new wooden bridge,

FROM LEFT It is hard to imagine soaking in the deep pools when the creek is high; the falls viewed from the north side of Perseverance Creek.

complete with handrails. The broad, gravel trail you are now on follows the creek only a short distance before heading to an open meadow ahead.

7. Overshadowed by large cottonwoods, the meadow (Coal Creek Historic Park) has a history of settlement and many newly built recreational features – including a disc-golf course, mounted photos and informative signs of early Chinese settlers, a picnic shelter and a large map of the whole network of trails.

8. While you might want to go as far as the picnic shelter and sign, turn back for the trail to complete your loop. Turn

left a short distance back on the aptly named (but unsign-posted) Swamp Trail leading along the shore of a pond. Seasonally bristling with cattails, the pond should be on your left. After you pass the end of the pond, there is another, close-up map sign and information about the community forest. It is tempting to go straight ahead on the large trail heading uphill – but make sure you don't miss the smaller trail on your left to keep close to the swamp until you have reached the far end.

9. As you climb away from the end of the swamp, you find yourself on the crest of a small ridge, and a somewhat unclear dirt area where the trail seems to disappear. Keep to your left to drop down off the end of the ridge and begin the last leg of your route on the Mama Bear mountain-biking trail.

10. After a few minutes of climbing, and then descending, come back to the large junction where you began your loop walk. Turn left to cross the bridge and walk along Sutton Road back to your vehicle.

16. ROYSTON GHOST SHIP TRAIL

*A broad, level, seaside trail with excellent views
of the Royston Wrecks, or ghost ships, and, across
Courtenay Harbour to Goose Spit.*

LOCATION
Heading north on Highway 19A through Royston, measure 2 km
from the bridge over the Trent River and turn right onto Hilton
Road. Follow it a short distance to its end.

If you are driving south from Courtenay on Highway 19A,
Hilton Road is 3 km from the traffic light at the Comox Valley
Parkway intersection. In either case, notice a blue and white sign
for Royston Seaside Trail.

DISTANCE
2.2-km return

ELEVATION GAIN
None

DIFFICULTY
Easy, broad surface of crushed gravel. Extending the walk along
the intertidal zone is a little more difficult since the surface
is sometimes slippery, especially in winter and early spring.
Some children, no doubt, will want to explore the breakwater
and rusted ships. However, at this writing, the approach to the
breakwater is fenced off.

SEASON
All season

OF SPECIAL INTEREST FOR CHILDREN

The words "ghost ships" are used in local lingo to describe the broken hulks of ships forming part of a breakwater – what better way to provoke a sense of mystery and romance? Kids who prefer to ride their bikes while their parents walk will find the going easy along the trail. A small beach by the parking lot, can, of course, provide various watery diversions. Interpretative signs give some interesting history and understanding of the trail.

1. The well-designed parking and turnaround area has facilities including interpretative signs and an outhouse. While this is essentially a T-shaped trail, with branches going both north and south from this spot, the main continuous trail runs north along the shore. Before hitting the trail, make your way to the shore where you get a good view of the ghost-ship breakwater from slightly north of the breakwater itself.

2. Turn back and head right along the signposted trail with the ocean on your right. You soon find a sign announcing the waterside strip of land has been closed off because of "dangerous caverns." The trail passes behind a swampy pond that provides habitat for many critters.

3. Returning to the seaside bank, you come upon a park bench. This next section of the trail is backed by houses, fortunately set well back from the trail. Pause to read the interesting interpretative sign headed "Where Land Meets Sea," with information on a "green shores" approach to preventing further erosion from the tides.

4. The next section runs a little inland behind a screen of thimbleberry, blackberry and wild rose thickets. When the trail again joins the shore, you come to another park bench and an interpretative sign explaining the logging history behind the trail – including the extraordinary construction of a mile-long pier.

FROM LEFT One of the ghost ships along the breakwater, and bird houses for purple martins on the pilings; the level gravel trail makes for easy strolling. Comox is across Courtenay Harbour.

5. When you reach the signposted end of the trail at Chinook Road, return to your starting point. Cross the parking area and go a short distance to the south of the breakwater. Ignore a trail branching off to the right (giving access to Lince Road). The main advantage of following this short trail is being able to get a particularly good view of the breakwater and ships, this time from the south with the sunlight behind illuminating the wrecks and rocks.

Optional Add-On: Bank-Top Trail

As you have seen from the posted map at the parking spot, the recommended route has you walking along the shore for a hundred or so metres to rejoin another small section of bank-top trail. If you do take this option and go the extra distance, spot picnic tables and a viewing platform leading out and over the upper shore.

17. TRENT RIVER FALLS

A magnificent single-drop falls in a canyon of nearly sheer walls of shale, within easy walking distance of the highway.

LOCATION

Four kilometres south of the Courtenay/Cumberland exits on the Inland Highway (19). Driving south, park just off the road near the bridge. A large sign here warns against fires.

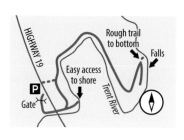

DISTANCE

1 km, but seems longer because of the variety

ELEVATION GAIN

30 m

DIFFICULTY

The user-made trail is mostly easy, but parents should keep their children close to them since, like many falls in the area, this one has a steep, potentially dangerous descent to the base of the canyon. Only older, sure-footed children should venture beyond the viewpoints.

SEASON

The raging power of the falls in winter can diminish to little more than a trickle by summer's end – but in all seasons the setting and changing character give the walk a magical atmosphere.

OF SPECIAL INTEREST FOR CHILDREN

The falls can be magnificent and awe-inspiring if they are full. In the pool below the falls, bodies of salmon can be seen in autumn since they can make the journey this far up the river, but no farther.

Since this is not in a park, trails are not necessarily maintained, though they are well-travelled in warm weather by those going to the swimming hole.

It is possible to make a shortcut to the falls by parking on the east side of the highway or walking across the highway and making your way across a ditch about 30 m from the bridge. Here you see an old roadbed going straight ahead into small alders.

The recommended route, however, starts on the other side of the highway, as described under "Location," since starting on that side takes you easily by a side trail to the riverbank below some monumental slate cliffs.

---

1. Avoiding the ATV tracks close to the fire warning sign, walk towards the bridge, pass by the metal gates and descend on a clear trail below the bridge. Walk past the area of bare dirt under the bridge and, picking up a trail, descend towards the river. If you have brought young children, be aware that this is the only spot at which they can easily reach the river's edge. The beach of gravel and small rocks beside the gurgling water makes a pleasant place to visit and do a little manic splashing.

2. Return up the bank to find a newly made trail on the right that leads through some small trees. In fact, this trail runs almost parallel to the highway, though a little away from it. After a short distance, you arrive at a T junction with a much broader, established trail. Turn right.

3. Follow the flagged route along this broad trail, with the riverbank on your right and a lower, often damp area on your left. Once under the larger trees, notice small side trails leading to viewpoints down into the river gorge far below. Unfortunately, the tree cover makes it difficult to catch much more than a glimpse of the river.

4. The trail descends a few metres to a junction. To view the falls from an upstream vantage point, turn right. Although

CLOCKWISE FROM LEFT The falls viewed from the bank below the main pool; a small trail leads to a good viewpoint immediately above the falls; the shore by the easiest trail near the highway overpass.

this trail is not long, it does take you upstream from the falls and provides a few reasonably clear view spots onto the rock formations that form the steps over which the water begins its tumultuous – or in summer, decorous – descent. Overhanging branches screen your view a little, but, in the right mood, you can think of them as framing it!

5. Returning to the junction, look for the beginning of the track to the base of the falls – more precisely, the riverbank downstream from the falls. This is the trail used by brave (and sure-footed) souls in summer months to reach the pool at the base of the falls.

6. Return to your vehicle along the same route.

18. ROSEWALL CREEK

A creekside trail through Rosewall Creek Park,
under beautiful mixed forest of large maple, fir and hemlock.
The trail rises and dips after leaving the park,
ending with a view of pretty falls.

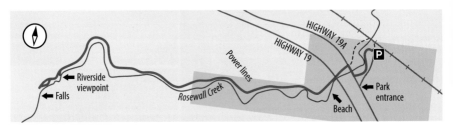

LOCATION
From Highway 19 near Bowser, take the Cook Creek exit (#87). Turn north on Highway 19A and drive 1.7 km, until you see the sign for Rosewall Creek Provincial Park. If you are driving south on 19A, look for the signposted park 6 km south of the Fanny Bay turnoff. Park in the main lot for the park.

DISTANCE
6.5-km return

ELEVATION GAIN
Cumulatively, about 170 m, depending on where you turn back, with high point of 130 m

DIFFICULTY
Most of the trail is easy, though a few wet crossings, eroded banks and rooty sections can make parents' lives interesting. The second part of the trail, outside park boundaries, has been maintained by Comox District Mountaineering Club. Ropes have been strung as assists on two fairly steep sections of trail. The last short section to the high viewpoint onto the falls is difficult and potentially unsafe.

SEASON

All season, though mud can be an unwelcome feature. The flow is quite good through to the end of a hot summer, but, unsurprisingly, the waterfall is most spectacular in wet seasons.

OF SPECIAL INTEREST FOR CHILDREN

A deep pool near the beginning of the trail is an obvious magnet. In the fall, the creek has spawning coho salmon. The pretty waterfall at the end of the trail is the main highlight, especially if your family is "collecting" waterfalls. Binoculars might be good, since the falls can be most securely viewed from downstream rather than from the last section of difficult trail.

1. Begin with the wheelchair-accessible short loop trail through the main area of the park, possibly taking advantage of picnic tables and outhouses.

2. Follow the creekside trail to the highway and cross the bridge, dropping down a trail towards the creek and walking under the highway.

3. The first section of the trail, within provincial park land, soon leads to a pleasant beach opposite a clay cliff. The trail soon swings away from the creek, crosses two places that can be wet and brings you to a creekside pile of fallen trees, deposited there during flooding. Here is a good educational opportunity to point out the destructive damage of erosion and flooding.

4. The trail turns away from the creek and rises above a flood plain before dipping close to the creek. Children might be interested in a huge cedar stump, with not one but two sets of historic springboard holes from early logging days. The stump also functions as a nursery for small hemlocks. Make your way past two eroded sections of trail and, if you like, take a short exploratory trail down to a gravel bar before returning to the main trail. The trail climbs slightly until it reaches a sign indicating the provincial park boundary.

FROM LEFT Even when the summer water level is lowest, the creek has enticing, clear pools; while a difficult trail leads to the distant falls, this view spot makes for a good family-hike destination.

5. A rope-assisted descent brings the trail to the stream and soon to the beginning of the longest section of trail close to the stream. A fairly long climb and rope-assisted bit of trail takes you high above the stream before bringing you again down to stream level. Take the side trail to the creek and the best view spot for looking upstream to the falls.

6. Only the most sure-footed should venture farther. Climbing to the best viewpoint requires ducking through logs and passing rooty, steep trail with some potentially dangerous drops. If you do venture here, the route farther away from the creek is generally easier and safer.

7. Return the way you came.

19. LIGHTHOUSE COUNTRY TRAIL & WILDWOOD TRAIL

A beautiful, winding forest walk through the endangered Coastal Douglas Fir Ecosystem, passing many character trees.

LOCATION

A little south of downtown Bowser on Highway 19A, look for a blue and white sign pointing towards both Wildwood Community Trail and Lighthouse Country Trail. Turn onto McColl Road and drive about 300 m. Cross the railway tracks and park in the signposted little parking lot. Similar signs are situated farther south on Charlton Drive and Lions Drive, but these are for the South Loop trail (see trip 20).

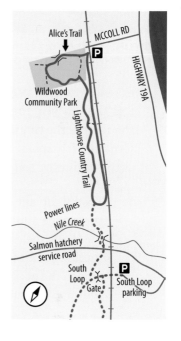

DISTANCE

2.7-km loop

ELEVATION GAIN

Negligible

DIFFICULTY

Easy, but since it is quite rooty in places, and requires walking over some split logs at damp areas, it is not as easy as the sister trail immediately south with its wheelchair-accessible, broad, gravel trail.

SEASON

All season, but there can be some fairly large puddles in winter.

OF SPECIAL INTEREST FOR CHILDREN

This is a good trail to set up some treasure-hunt goals for children who don't see much point in simply walking. For such children, ask them to count bridges, look for the giant Douglas fir,

FROM LEFT Some large cedars and rustic bridges add charm to Wildwood Trail; the narrow trail winds amongst large, second-growth forest.

the most twisted fairy-tale tree, the (signposted) "hugging log" and the bracket, fungus-covered giant, dead tree. Best of all, though, are the tiny plastic critters that peep out from moss and ferns at a few spots. When all else fails, there is the picnic table at the beginning and end of the hike!

1. Go straight ahead down the crushed gravel trail, over a little bridge and come to a junction. It's worth reading the sign about the endangered Coastal Douglas Fir Ecosystem, if nothing else to heighten the appreciation of the flora and fauna in the park. Turn right to begin your loop through the Wildwood Community Park part of the overall loop.

2. Pass the Lighthouse Country Trail sign and, within a few steps, come to the sign for Alice's Trail. Turn left and pass a sign for Wildwood Community Park, climbing slightly and crossing a small bridge. Ignore a trail to the left leading across another little bridge. When you come to a fork, notice a sign for Alice's Trail and arrows pointing in both directions – confusingly ambiguous. Take the left fork.

3. At another fork in a short distance, prepare for the same situation: a sign for Alice's Trail that is not at all clear about where it points. Again, take the left fork. After a short distance you come to a kind of T junction. Straight ahead you can see a cross trail, but turn right to follow the sign saying "Lighthouse Country Trail." (Actually, there are two: a new blue sign and an older green one.)

Occasionally, the trail can be rooty and damp.

4. This next section of the trail is probably the most beautiful, zigzagging and passing many striking trees, comparatively small hemlocks and often larger cedars, as well as one huge Douglas fir. Also keep your eyes open for a few tufts of deer fern, unusual on the east coast of the island. En route, cross little bridges and boardwalks, testifying to the care that has gone into constructing the trail.

5. When the trail approaches the end of the forested strip, it turns sharp left. Ignore a trail to the right leading a short distance to the power lines. Follow the trail parallel to the power lines, en route admiring the care that has gone into cobbling some of the otherwise muddy sections of trail.

6. Turn left when you reach the end of this section to follow the nearly straight-as-a-die trail back to your starting point. En route, pass several side trails to your right leading to the railway tracks running parallel to your route. Also pass (a little confusingly) a sign with arrows pointing to an unnamed trail to the left. Ignore this and carry on straight ahead on Lighthouse Country Trail until you reach your car.

20. LIGHTHOUSE COUNTRY REGIONAL TRAIL, SOUTH LOOP

More than 2 km of winding wheelchair- (and stroller-) accessible trail through pretty trees with the option of a return route through varied terrain.

LOCATION

At the northern end of Qualicum Bay (not to be confused with Qualicum Beach, many kilometres south), along Highway 19A, notice the blue and white sign for the trail and an indication to turn onto Charlton Drive. About 400 m along turn left onto Linx Road and drive about 400 m to a large circular area just before the railway tracks. Park here, walk across the railway tracks a short distance to the signposted entrance to the trail. The outhouse here just might be of interest. The name of the trail comes from the fact that this section of coast calls itself Lighthouse Country (because of two lighthouses visible across the waters).

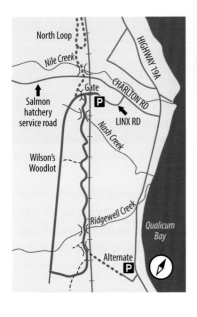

DISTANCE
2.5 km

ELEVATION GAIN
Negligible

DIFFICULTY
As easy a trail as you will find anywhere, level, with a crushed-gravel surface. The trail even has a tapping edge, designed to

allow visually impaired visitors to navigate easily. The optional return loop is much more uneven, sometimes rooty and occasionally muddy.

SEASON
All season, and blessedly free of wet spots.

OF SPECIAL INTEREST FOR CHILDREN
This is a perfect trail for kids whose enthusiasm for walking is a tad less than their joy on two wheels. A picnic table strategically placed halfway along the easy part of the trail is also helpful.

1. Cross a metal bridge over Nash Creek and begin a long section of artfully winding trail. En route to the picnic spot, pass a wooden bridge and two benches. You also pass a trail leading to the right that you should ignore. Although the forest along this section is primarily the familiar mix of cedar and fir, when you get to the picnic area, notice the interpretative sign for Sitka spruce, rare on the east coast of the island.

2. Along the second half of this lovely trail you pass two more benches, and two more wooden bridges, the first one over Ridgewell Creek, the second over one of its tributaries. Between the two bridges is a track leading to your right that you should ignore. Almost immediately thereafter you come to a significant fork. Assess the needs of your troupe, since there is a washroom a few metres down the trail left, at the south trailhead and parking lot.

3. If you want the easiest and prettiest way back, simply return the way you came. If you want a little more adventure and variety, turn right at the fork. This comparatively small dirt connector trail takes you through a forest primarily of large fir and hemlock. This trail is more challenging for bicycles, though passable for those of an intermediate level. At your first fork, turn left on the larger trail, though the right fork

CLOCKWISE FROM ABOVE LEFT The meticulously prepared trail has rustic benches, boardwalks and a tapping rail for the visually impaired; an aluminum bridge and signposts make the main part of the route easy to use; the bridge over Nile Creek for those who follow the optional trail to the North Loop.

circles around and rejoins the main trail. Turning left again, therefore, at the second fork, go a short distance to a third fork. This time turn right, ignoring the trail forking left and going over a small bridge.

4. When you get to a T junction with Wilson Woodlot Road (unsignposted), turn right. This road goes through a private forest, and at this writing it has been closed (only temporarily) while foresters are at work. Approximately two-thirds of the way along this pretty gravel road ignore a fork to the right (leading to the wheelchair-friendly trail).

5. Once you have closed the loop, and if you have lots of curiosity and vigour, you can make your way to the North Loop along a volunteer-made route. If, however, you have been on bicycles until this point, you now must leave them at your car.

Optional Add-On: The North Loop

Just before reaching the yellow gate and directly opposite the blue and white sign for Woodlot Trail, take the trail over a tiny bridge. A short distance ahead, ignore the trail to the left (Dale's Trail) and go straight ahead to a fork. Take either fork, since both reconnect towards the bottom of the fairly steep, rooty, bank trail. Cross a small bridge to meet a well-used gravel road, leading to a fish hatchery and a wonderful hike up Nile Creek Falls. This hike is described in Popular Day Hikes 4: Vancouver Island. *Cross the road to take a well-built wooden bridge by some magnificent cedars and follow a switchbacking and comparatively fresh trail up the bank. At a T junction with a broader track, turn left, and within a minute or two come to another T junction, this time with a service road under the power lines. Cross the service road and take the well-built trail through the scrubby vegetation under the power lines to enter the trees and find yourself at the south end of the North Loop trail.*

21. HORNE LAKE CAVES & PHIL WHITFIELD INTERPRETIVE TRAIL

A suspension bridge and sequence of switchbacking climbs and staircases through forests via several cave entrances and a treasure trove of interpretive signs and diagrams. Guided tours or a self-guided tour of the main cave here in Horne Lake Caves Provincial Park is possible for those who are prepared – properly prepared – and are willing to take responsibility for older and capable children. The park website gives a chockablock list of advice.

LOCATION

At a set of traffic lights on Highway 19, 22 km north of Parksville (63 km south of Courtenay), a prominent sign points the way to Horne Lake Caves Provincial Park. Turn onto Horne Lake Road (Exit 75), and about 13.5 km along you come to the park with its many facilities. Drive past the camping areas, following the signs for the caves entrance.

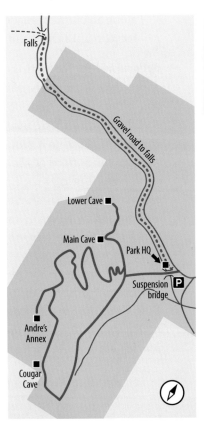

DISTANCE

2.1 km, mostly a loop

ELEVATION GAIN

70 m, cumulative

DIFFICULTY

A well-maintained park trail with strong, well-protected bridges and

Suspension bridge over the Qualicum River to the trailhead.

high staircases and walkways. Very young children may need help up some of the longest climbs.

SEASON
All season

OF SPECIAL INTEREST FOR CHILDREN
For most children, caves are inherently fascinating. The fact that they can visit the entrances to caves and sinkholes and even poke their noses inside will be enough to interest them. To the main course of these features, add the spice of a long suspension bridge approach and the many illustrated signs explaining features of the formation of caves.

1. The large parking area adjoins washrooms and a building where helmets and lights can be rented (during park hours)

for those who want to do a little self-exploration or arrange for a guided tour of otherwise inaccessible caves. Assuming you are going to stick to the trail, walk towards and cross the large suspension bridge over the deliciously clear waters of the Qualicum River. Go straight ahead uphill to a junction of signposted trails under a canopy of maples.

2. Turn right, onto the trail to Lower Cave. Although this is not part of the loop, the trail has many interesting features that make it a worthwhile out-and-back tromp. First, pass some dramatic limestone cliffs overhung with ferns and mosses and a set of stairs leading to signposted Main Cave. If – and only if – you are properly prepared (see the park's website for advice), you can venture into this cave.

3. Return to the walkway, skirting the flank of the steep forested slope, towards a sequence of suspended wooden staircases, dropping impressively through the trees. Follow a suspended boardwalk around a corner and more stairs to bring you to the gated and forbidding entrance to Lower Cave.

4. Return to the first signposted junction and the trail leading to Riverbend Cave. This initiates a series of fact-filled signs, beginning with an explanation of the formation of limestone or karst from ancient seashells. A series of nine switchbacks leads you up the forested slope and, after several interpretative signs, brings you to the imagination-gripping explanation of sinkholes.

5. Continue past Riverbend Cave, just a few steps off the main trail, and, in sequence, the short trail to Andre's Annex and Cougar Cave, with its chilling warning about a "hazardous blind pit" and the nearby explanation of "epikarst."

6. The descending part of the trail includes one section of wooden staircase, but otherwise curves gently and consistently down the slope of small firs to rejoin the entrance trail and the short walk to the suspension bridge.

CLOCKWISE FROM LEFT Elaborate staircases and boardwalks near the caves; one of the many boardwalks through the park; the falls can be visited as part of an optional walk along the gravel road.

Optional Add-On: Upstream to the Falls and Rapids

When you return to your car, you may wish to walk (or cycle) 2 km upstream along the forestry road. The road is exceptionally quiet – expect not to see a single vehicle – and walking it allows for some wonderful roadside views through the trees of the crystal-clear waters of the Qualicum River, rushing over the boulders and through deep green pools. The climax of the walk is a beautiful sequence of falls and rapids, twisting and splashing through sculpted rock formations under a wooden bridge. Yes, this side trip is highly recommended.

22. HORNE LAKE & RIVER LOOP

A combination of trails within the network of Horne Lake Regional Park's trails, allowing access to the most attractive parts of the pebbly lakeshore and, later, views across the Qualicum River to the twisted rock faces above the lake.

LOCATION

At a set of traffic lights on Highway 19, 22 km north of Parksville (63 km south of Courtenay), at Exit 75, a prominent sign points the way to Horne Lake Caves Provincial Park. Turn onto Horne Lake Road and about 13.5 km along come to Horne Lake Regional Park with its various facilities. Follow the signs over the bridge to Twin Pines Campground. Just before your destination is a sign on your left, pointing to Viewpoint Trail. Don't be tempted to explore this trail unless you fancy a mindless slog up an old road to a dead end with nothing very much that even approximates a "view." Instead, park in the signposted parking lot on your left.

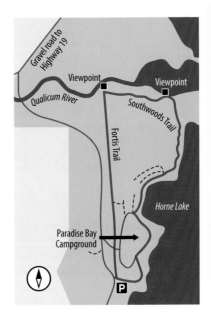

DISTANCE
2.5 km

ELEVATION GAIN
Negligible

DIFFICULTY
Easy park trail, though some sections are rooty.

SEASON

All season, but come during warm weather to combine walking with water play. The lake can get warm.

OF SPECIAL INTEREST FOR CHILDREN

The lovely sweep of pebble beach with picnic tables near the beginning of the loop can be an enticement to be visited at the end of the walk.

1. From the parking area just off to the left of the through road, walk straight ahead (noting the possibly useful outhouses), and take the track to the campground. Turn right to follow the campground road past the tent sites on either side, some of them perfectly situated on the shore of the lake. (Perhaps note a favourite site yourself for your own future camping visit!)

2. At the north end of the looping campground road, pass another parking area and washroom, and go straight ahead past a yellow post. Of the three trailheads close to each other ahead, take the first one you come to, labelled "Southwoods Trail."

3. Almost immediately find yourself in an attractive forest, primarily of substantial cedar. While the trail is generally clear, any ambiguity is offset by small orange diamonds nailed onto trees. The trail runs immediately parallel to and close by the shore, though mostly behind a screen of trees.

4. When you come to a junction of other trails (including Alder Loop), forge ahead past the sign pointing you onwards on Southwoods Trail. After some distance close to the lake, the trail cuts inland and suddenly emerges onto the gravelly estuary of the Qualicum River as it empties into Horne Lake. The views across the estuary and onto the twisted strata of limestone in the rock faces opposite are particularly punchy photo ops.

CLOCKWISE FROM TOP LEFT The fine pebble beach and stratified cliffs; the view across the estuary; the estuary at the mouth of the Qualicum River where the trail turns upstream.

5. Follow the trail roughly parallel to the banks of the river, but largely away from it, until you come to a second viewpoint with a good view of the clear pools and intersecting channels in the slow-moving river. This section of trail can be a little bushy, as it runs by a recently logged area now covered with small alders and salal.

6. Notice the blue park sign pointing sharp left down a razor-straight, wide, grassy strip cut through the trees. The trail is the namesake of Fortis, the natural gas company, which explains why it is so straight and wide.

7. This part of your route leads straight ahead back to your car. En route, you pass a gravel road leading to your left and a blue sign confirming that the straight-ahead trail is Fortis Trail. Just before the parking lot, the trail crosses another gravel road, this one the signposted entrance to Paradise Bay Campground. It's called that for a reason.

23. BIG QUALICUM RIVER

A series of trails through some large trees, running parallel to the Big Qualicum River and the fish hatching channel, with the possibility of viewing spawning salmon.

LOCATION

From the Inland Island Highway (19) near Qualicum Bay, turn towards the ocean (east) at the Horne Lake Road intersection (Exit 75) and drive 2.2 km. Turn left onto River Road and drive for 800 m. Notice the sign for the Big Qualicum Fish Hatchery. Turn left into the parking lot.

DISTANCE

6-km loop (with options)

ELEVATION GAIN

40 m

DIFFICULTY

Mostly easy, broad tracks, with one section on a quiet service road. Two single-log bridges over the river have good grip underfoot and hand support. There are lots of warnings posted alerting you to the possibility of crossing paths with Mr. Bear during spawning season in the fall.

SEASON

All season, but most interesting during spawning season. Can be a little smelly for the month after spawning season when salmon carcasses are stacked at spots along the river. Autumn colours can be gorgeous since bigleaf maples are everywhere.

OF SPECIAL INTEREST FOR CHILDREN

Depending on which route you choose, bicycles (with solid tires) can be used. On the walking route suggested, the log bridges can intrigue children with a sense of adventure. The spawning salmon are a big draw, especially since near the trailhead there is a lot of interpretative information – including an under-water viewing building where kids can watch salmon swimming upstream against the current from a salmon's-eye view.

1. From the parking lot, follow the signs through the buildings to Big Qualicum River Regional Trail. Pause to look at the interpretative signs for the spawning channels. During spawning season, you may want to take a detour to the signposted entrance to the viewing area. Here you can drop below the level of the river and view the salmon swimming as they make their way up a concrete spawning channel.

2. Cross the river on the large service road and turn upstream to your left. In a short distance, come to signs on a post pointing across two metal bridges. Follow the sign pointing to Cutthroat Trail and Steelhead Trail over the bridge. Turn right onto Cutthroat Trail. This next section of trail is on a long, narrow island, with the spawning channel on your left and the main river on your right – though both look very much like rivers! As you head upstream, the broad dirt track runs alternately by the two banks. Pass under some magnificent large trees, including cedars and some of the biggest spruce to be found on the island's east coast. Pass two metal bridges on your right, leading to the service road across the river.

3. As you approach the tip of the island, swing left to follow the signs for "Steelhead Trail" across an easy log bridge. Turn upstream on the much narrower and more irregular Steelhead Trail. As you pass the tip of the island, look back at a large, purely functional bridge connecting the island to the service road.

CLOCKWISE FROM TOP LEFT The log bridge at the upstream end of the loop; a giant maple near the southern end of the riverside trail; deep pools and weirs make the Big Qualicum River good spawning territory.

4. Crossing a small wooden bridge, notice the split in the trail. Ignore the trail on the left. Carry on straight ahead, on a comparatively narrow trail, passing under the huge concrete bridge carrying the traffic of the Inland Island Highway above you.

5. Cross several small wooden bridges in succession, two of them made from fallen logs (but furnished with good surfaces.) Walk through an open area under power lines and enter the woods. After passing through comparatively small firs and alders, with a seasonal pond on your left, you eventually come to a white handmade sign on a small cedar, announcing "bridge" to the right, and, straight ahead, "Big Cedar 500 meters." Look right to see a more official signpost.

6. To visit a wonderful large cedar, go straight ahead, ignoring a small side trail on the left with a bit of orange flagging tape. When you've reached the tree, hugged it and taken your photos, you have reached the end of this bit of trail.

7. Return to the junction with the big tree trail and follow the sign towards Big Qualicum River Trail. This log bridge is a little more adventurous than the one lower down, since first you have to climb up two half logs onto a huge boulder, and then cross the river, this time with the assistance of a single hand support. For all but the smallest children, though, the crossing is safe and secure, with an excellent surface. Besides, it's fun.

8. Once across the river, take the right fork in the trail and, after a few minutes, climb the bank to Big Qualicum River Regional Trail, looking for all the world like the broad gravel fisheries service road that it actually is. Turn to the right, now heading downstream with the main river on your right.

9. After passing under the highway bridge, come to a smaller service road on your right by a bleakly serviceable looking building, opposite the upstream end of the island, along which runs Cutthroat Trail. Follow the sign to Spawning Channel Service Road. This track runs satisfyingly close to the fast-flowing water all the way back to the downstream end of the island.

10. The clearest route from here back to your car is back along the large service road the way you came. It is, however, possible to cross the large metal bridge to Steelhead Trail. If you take this option, turn left and make your way down a narrow and rooty trail past smaller spawning channels, then a large fence, ultimately joining a gravel maintenance road that leads back to the visitor parking lot.

Optional Add-On: Steelhead Trail towards Horne Lake
If you have brought bicycles with sturdy tires, follow the directions only to the upstream tip of the island, since Steelhead Trail is too rough and narrow for most children to ride. From the north tip of the island, cross to Big Qualicum River Regional Trail and turn left, upstream, to ride for as many kilometres as you like towards Horne Lake. On your return leg, turn right at the service building and follow the signs for Spawning Channel Service Road in order to follow the most pleasant, waterside route back to the parking lot.

24. PACIFIC RIM NATIONAL PARK FOREST TRAILS

The several seaside trails of Pacific Rim Park are described in my *Seaside Walks of Vancouver Island*. The trails described here are all short inland trails, beautiful and awe-inspiring, often over-looked, easily visited singly or in any combination.

A. Shorepine Bog Trail

Probably the most distinctive – and bizarre – easily accessible trail on Vancouver Island. A continuous boardwalk loop through desert-like, stunted and exotic-looking vegetation. Lots of interpretative signs.

LOCATION
From the Pacific Rim National Park Visitor Centre on Highway 4, drive towards Tofino for 4.8 km. Turn left onto Wick Road (also signposted for Wickaninnish Interpretive Centre). After 1.6 km, turn into the signposted parking area.

DISTANCE
800-m loop

ELEVATION GAIN
Negligible

DIFFICULTY
One of the only wheelchair- and stroller-accessible trails in the park. Entirely on boardwalk suspended above the bog.

SEASON
All season

OF SPECIAL INTEREST FOR CHILDREN
Although most kids have difficulty in sustaining interest in flora, the route is short, the boardwalk is inherently fun, the interpretive signs have genuinely interesting information and, most of all, it is easy to hype the vegetation as "Martian," "magic," "fantasy" and so on.

FROM LEFT Otherworldly forests of shore pine grow in the wet, acidic soil; many of the trees are like natural bonsais.

Directions are unnecessary for the trail since there are no choices to be made. You might, however, want to know in advance that the highly acidic nature of the soil has been created by water accumulating rather than draining. The thick layer of sphagnum moss and gnarled, stunted umbrella pines (some 300 years old) and twisted yellow cedars dotted around the almost treeless bog produce a hauntingly otherworld effect.

B. Rainforest Trails

Giant, ancient cedars and hemlocks overshadow a jungle gym of suspended boardwalk, twisting, climbing and dropping through a fantastical ancient treescape.

LOCATION
Drive towards Tofino on Highway 4, going about 6 km from the Pacific Rim Park Visitor Centre (or just over a kilometre from the turnoff to Shorepine Bog Trail [above]), until you see the large national park sign for the parking lot on the left. Note there is a washroom and a map posted here.

DISTANCE
Two loops, each about 1 km long, on either side of the highway

ELEVATION GAIN

About 100 m, cumulative, with many rises and drops along a sequence of wooden stairs

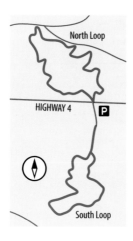

DIFFICULTY

Technically, the trail could hardly be easier, given the boardwalks and stairs. Wood, however, can be slippery when wet and stairs can be tiring, especially for little legs. At many – but not all – points a single handrail gives a little support and protection.

SEASON

All season, but avoid frosty (or snowy!) conditions.

OF SPECIAL INTEREST FOR CHILDREN

The fantastical shapes of some of the trees and the sheer fun of clambering along steps and boardwalks above the forest will intrigue most kids. In the fall there is the additional chance of seeing the odd spawning coho salmon. Many interpretative signs dot the trail, some of which could interest curious children.

1. Turn down the trail on the side of the highway where you are parked. After a section of crushed gravel, the trail becomes wooden boardwalk.

2. When you come to a split, turn left and follow the descending trail curving and turning on raised boardwalk, sometimes past some particularly weird and wonderful clusters of twisted and deformed trees and banks of deer fern. Generally following the side of a ravine with a stream below, the route crosses bridges. One, along a giant log, is especially memorable.

3. Heading back towards the parking lot, be prepared to climb up lots of wooden stairs. This side of the loop has few spots where you can look out over the forest and, if you like, become just a little...transported.

FROM LEFT Amazingly complex boardwalks wind past a giant cedar; from many viewpoints the boardwalks stretch far into the distance.

4. Back at the junction, return the way you came.

5. Cross the highway, trying not to risk life and limb, to begin the second loop, this one with almost no repeated sections. Turn left, and begin the comparatively ordinary bit of the walk, roughly parallel to the highway, before heading farther away from the sound of traffic.

6. Descend to the first of many impressive sets of steps leading down and winding through bushes. When you come to a short trail on your left, pause to appreciate the sheer size of some of the trees near here. One, described as an "Ancient Monarch" is accompanied by a special viewing platform and an interpretative sign dating it back to its beginning as a sapling in 1271.

7. Again the trail continues to rise and descend before climbing and leading to another side trail, this one with views of a creek – usually running, even through the summer. More flights of steps and a short walk bring you back to your car.

25. TONQUIN TRAIL

A gravel trail on the outskirts of Tofino winding through richly varied rainforest to high headlands and sandy Pacific beaches.

LOCATION
From Campbell Street, the main street in Tofino, turn onto 1st Street and drive for just under 0.5 km. Turn left onto Arnet Road and go about 150 m, to Tofino Community Hall. Park where you see an outhouse, a posted map and the trailhead.

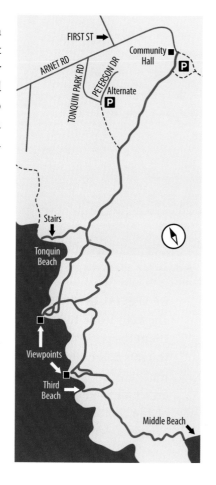

DISTANCE
3.8-km return

ELEVATION GAIN
60 m, cumulative, over many lumps and bumps

DIFFICULTY
The trail itself is well prepared and has a generally smooth surface. There are a few slopes in the trail and a sizeable set of (sturdy) stairs leading down to the beach. Small children will need help getting down the eroded bank onto Tonquin Beach.

SEASON
All season, with only a few wet spots in the wet season.

Arrive at low tide to visit the tiny islet on Tonquin Beach.

OF SPECIAL INTEREST FOR CHILDREN

The trail leads to two gorgeous, sandy beaches. (Three if you count the pocket-sized Third Beach.) Need any more be said? The water is nearly always on the nippy side of nippy, but, that aside, there are few more beautiful beaches...anywhere. While bicycles aren't allowed on the trail, immediately next to the beginning of the trail is an enticing mountain-bike park with ramps and bridges aplenty.

1. The first part of the trail, on a well-graded gravel base, takes you through comparatively light, open forest looking a little like an ornamental garden. After dipping and rising it brings you to a large gravel area where you see a sign and a trail leading a short distance to an alternative entrance to the trails (off Peterson Drive).

2. Pick up the onward trail and enter a forest of larger trees, mostly cedar, hemlock and spruce. When you come to a signpost and junction, take the right fork and go the short distance to an impressive raised wooden staircase. From the bottom of the stairs, turn right to find the best way down the eroding bank to the beach. Once on the beach, notice a few metres to the right another trailhead, this one for a trail favoured by locals as the shortest way to the beach. The beach is protected by islands from the huge waves that crash around and along most of the coast here and, unlike most beaches, has no dune area.

3. After exploring the beach, climb back up the stairs and return the short distance to the T junction with the posted map. Turn right, descend a little to cross a bridge, and come to another junction, this one for a loop trail. For now, turn right past a map and climb towards a headland on the south side of Tonquin Beach. If you're after a good view – and who isn't? – feel free to ignore the first small side trail dipping off the main trail on the right. It provides a pleasant little bit of exploration but comes to a dead end without much panache.

4. After climbing a little and descending, the main onward trail passes two quaintly hobbity benches. Planting yourself on the second one allows a lovely high perspective back onto the beach. Ahead, prepare yourself for some of the most amazingly rich nurse-log growth you are likely to find any-where. It would be criminal not to linger, photograph and/ or muse here. Next of interest on the agenda is a little side trail to the right, leading, as it turns out, only a short dis-tance to nowhere in particular.

5. When, however, just along a titch, you come to another fork and a signpost announcing a view in 50 m, do take it seri-ously. The entire end of the high promontory here bristles with cross trails and wooden structures suspended over the drop. The views in all directions have considerable Wow

CLOCKWISE FROM ABOVE An impressive viewing platform juts out over the cliffs; Third Beach; a glimpse of Clayoquot Sound.

factor and, because of the high perspective, are quite unlike any others in or around the national park.

6. If and when you've taken enough photos, swing back to the main through trail and turn right. The trail passes comparatively light and open forest, bringing you within minutes to another fork. There is absolutely no point in taking the left branch since the version on the right, running parallel to the main trail for a short distance, has infinitely more attractive views. The pocket beach of mixed sand and rock far below is the uninspiringly named Third Beach. From here you can glimpse the path to the beach itself at the far end of the tiny bay.

7. Return to the main trail, passing a pleasant but undramatic short trail to the right. Although you need to descend considerably to reach the shore of Third Beach, the slope is gradual and well-surfaced. En route, pass a fork to the left. After your exploration of the beach – best done at low tide – return to this fork and turn right for the final leg of the trail.

8. Mostly back from the water and viewpoints, this most-recently built chunk of trail (not shown on older maps) swerves, curves, dips and dives all the way to a long, broad and altogether typical Pacific Coast beach. Middle Beach is, to date, blessedly free from development except for a lodge, largely tucked into the trees at the far end. This beach makes for a great picnic and turnaround destination.

9. Retrace your route. However, when you get to the sign for the loop trail pointing right, add a little spice to your outing by exploring this alternative. The short loop rises over a crest before zigzagging a little and bringing you back to the main trail just before the bridge. Be sure to follow the correct signposts back to the community hall parking lot: some visitors have been known to become disoriented and even a little lost on their way home!

26. FOSSLI PARK

*A user-maintained provincial park, featuring
a spectacular suspension bridge, a pretty waterfall
and a picnic site by a small beach on Sproat Lake.*

LOCATION
Leaving Port Alberni on Highway 4 (towards
Tofino), cross the Somass River and, after
500 m, turn left onto McCoy Lake Road. Drive
for approximately 3 km and, at Stirling Arm
Drive, turn left. Keeping alert to a sharp turn,
go left to keep on this road and follow it for just
over 1.7 km until you reach an angled crossroads
with a gravel logging road (Ash Main). After just
under 1 km, and a T junction, turn right onto
another logging road (confusingly, another part
of Stirling Arm Drive). After about 3.8 km you
see a trailhead with a vertical signpost for Fossli
Trail and a small parking area on the right. If
you cross a bridge you have gone too far.

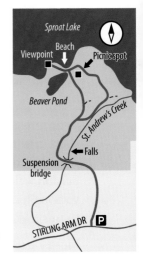

DISTANCE
3.8-km return with a loop

ELEVATION GAIN
80 m on return leg

DIFFICULTY
Generally easy to moderate but may need climbing over some wind-
fall. The waterfall is best viewed from St. Andrew's Creek streambed below the falls since the cliffs above the falls can be dangerous.

SEASON
All season, but obviously not equally good for all attractions all
year round.

The suspension bridge high over the Fossli Creek gorge.

OF SPECIAL INTEREST FOR CHILDREN

An impressively narrow (but secure) suspension bridge, coho salmon spawning in the fall, a pleasant beach with picnic spot. Fossli Trail is best visited on weekends, when you don't need to worry about logging-road traffic, or, at times, with getting permission to use the logging road.

1. The first section along an old logging road is a little uninspiring, descending fairly steeply through small alders and hemlocks towards the somewhat older forest and the park boundary. Ignore one track to the left and three to the right and look for the signposted main path just before the park boundary.

2. Follow the descending path to the suspension bridge high over a narrow, twisted gorge. Once across the bridge, you soon hear the falls, but, particularly with children, don't try to go beyond the guardrail towards more precipitous viewpoints. Instead, carry on along the descending trail, dropping off towards the creek below.

3. Descending to the flats, mostly below large maples, keep ahead on the main trail, ignoring branches off to the right towards

The trail leads to a beach on Sproat Lake.

St. Andrew's Creek. As you approach the lakeshore, note two trails to the right, but, for now, seek out a narrow trail to the left.

4. Take this small trail, sometimes a little overgrown, along a bluff a few metres above the lake, to a pretty viewpoint down the lake and towards a beaver pond. Drink in the prettiness, compose a little ode and return to the main trail.

5. Take the trail closer to the lake and go a short distance to a pretty beach and view across the lake. Pause here for watery pleasures or, if your family has…needs…take another little trail up from the beach to a picnic table, and farther up, a clearing and an outhouse.

6. While the main trail returns the way you came, you can make a loop by following the trail past the clearing. This comparatively narrow trail rises and drops twice before arriving at a T junction. Turn left and make your way towards the creek. While various small trails run through the flat area near the stream, taking the trails towards the stream will bring you to a good viewpoint up the stream to the pretty waterfall.

7. Turn back to join the trail that climbs uphill to join the main trail. From here, retrace your route.

27. WEINER FALLS

Easy access from a highway to a little-known but impressively high single-drop falls into a deep, treed gorge.

LOCATION
On Highway 4 to Tofino, near Sproat Lake, cross the bridge over the Sproat River and, after just under 4 km, look for Sproat Lake Landing Resort. Immediately opposite, turn right onto a gravel road and proceed for about 200 m. Take a left at the fork just before a bridge, identified with a yellow sign, and drive for about 500 m. It is probably best to park at a broad gravel patch opposite a road leading slightly uphill to the right, though it is possible to cut off a little of your walk by driving a short distance up this road.

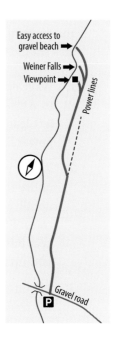

DISTANCE
2 km (from recommended parking spot)

ELEVATION GAIN
60 m

DIFFICULTY
The trail is mostly broad and easy (along an old roadbed), until the last section, though it does call for some climbing. The final sections of dirt trail to the falls are easy to walk, though one branch might require hopping over a small stream in winter. The route to the bottom of the falls from the view spot is extremely steep. Though used by many, and supplied with a less-than-new rope, it could be dangerous. Strict admonitions to children are probably appropriate!

SEASON

All season, though probably best in winter and early spring when the falls are fullest and when the leaves are off the branches that otherwise screen the best view of the falls.

OF SPECIAL INTEREST FOR CHILDREN

The dizzying sense of height and the sight of the beautiful, high falls should perk up even the most videogame-addicted child.

1. Walk up the little-used roadbed through trees and emerge to a cleared area under power lines. Ignore a track to your left leading downhill. Carry on uphill under and across the power lines, ignoring a track on the right.

2. When you reach the left (west) side of the cleared strip under the power lines, ignore the main track swinging right uphill, and turn onto a smaller one to the left entering the trees. Follow this track, roughly parallel to the power lines, up a fairly steep climb. Some visitors are known to huff and puff up this section.

3. As you become aware of the sound of rushing water through the trees, notice a small trail on your left. Ignore this dead-end path to the top of a steep bank. It has virtually no view. Carry on straight ahead to a clear split in the well-used trail. The trail to the right leads to two more trails, one to the very top of the falls, one a short distance upstream to a gravel bar and the creek itself.

4. Turn right and, at the next fork, turn left. Within a short distance, emerge to the dizzying sense of being at the very lip of the falls as they disappear and drop far, far below. Be careful if you try to get to a better viewpoint: the rock surfaces, even though they look flat, can be extremely slippery.

5. Return to the fork and turn left, upstream, along a newly made and carefully constructed bit of trail. In winter you must hop over a small tributary stream before going a short

FROM LEFT The falls are most safely viewed from the top of the bank, but a rough trail goes to the base; the trail ends at this small creekside spot, slightly upstream from the falls.

distance to the edge of the creek. The view upstream, as the clear water rushes down over the rocks, is particularly photographable.

6. Turn back to take the first fork to the viewpoint onto the face of the falls. You can see the falls from here well enough (especially when there are no leaves on the trees) that venturing farther is unnecessary. An extremely steep track drops over roots and rock to the pool at the bottom of the falls. While there is a rope in place to give some sense of security, the rope is not in good condition and a fall could be very, very messy.

7. Return the way you came.

28. STAMP RIVER – GREENMAX ANGLERS' TRAIL

*Originally used by fishermen along the southwest shore
of the fast-flowing, crystal-clear Stamp River,
past deep pools and rapids.*

LOCATION

Leaving Port Alberni behind you on Highway 4 as you drive towards Pacific Rim Park, cross a prominent bridge over the Somass River and, approximately 12 km along, a more dramatic high-level bridge over the same river. Shortly afterwards take the second turn right onto Coleman Road. Drive along this gravel road past the turn to the airport. Very soon after crossing a small creek, notice the yellow-gated logging road on the left and, beside it, parking for one car and a large, carefully presented map of Greenmax Anglers' Trail. (The trail takes its name from the Greenmax logging woodlot.)

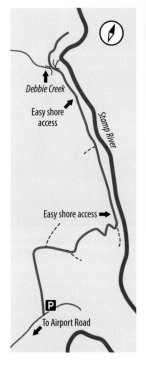

DISTANCE

4.8-km return

ELEVATION GAIN

110 m, cumulative

DIFFICULTY

Generally easy, but smaller children might have to be shepherded past a few spots where the fairly narrow trail drops off to the river.

SEASON

All season. Can be a little muddy in winter and spring. Even after a dry summer the river level tends to stay high enough to provide lots of visual splendour.

OF SPECIAL INTEREST FOR CHILDREN

It is possible – and enticing – to approach the river at two or three places for some splashing, but be aware that the river has some rapids downstream from some of these spots (see steps 5, 7 and 8 below).

1. Walk past the yellow gate and climb the hill, heading along the gravel road through a clear-cut area. Ignore a logging road leading to your right at the base of this hill. This exposed section can get hot under a blazing summer sun.

2. At the top of the hill take the right fork and enter a blessedly cool grove of fir, a few of them satisfyingly large and even a little bench.

3. Exit the grove and swing to the left, ignoring a short branch to the right. Soon reach the trailhead proper, entering a stand of small alder, fir and bracken.

4. Switchback down a moderately steep bank towards the river, and enter the stand of large, riverside fir, hemlock and cedar that will shadow the rest of your walk.

5. Ignore the broad trail/roadbed swinging downstream to your right. Instead, make your way straight ahead to the riverbank, even though, depending on the degree of spring flooding, the trail may be a little obscure for a few metres. This is one of the best spots to enjoy being immediately next to the river, though the water is rushing too vigorously at this point for this to be a great spot for children to get seriously involved with the water.

6. Turn upstream along the broad, sandy track, and almost immediately come to a picture-worthy, flat, rocky area protruding into the river and providing a perfect spot for soaking in the splendid view of rapids and the thickly forested bank opposite (including a dramatically leaning, huge fir).

FROM LEFT Rapids near the beginning of the trail; one of the deep, nearly still pools upstream along the path.

7. Next, the trail rises above the riverbank, within a few minutes passing some view spots of almost unbelievably deep, green pools with little trace of current except at high water. Pass a decaying plywood rain shelter erected by fishermen. There is a rough descent to the riverbank at this point.

8. Pass a trail leading to your left and a blue, spray-painted arrow pointing towards the "Woodlot" (and a logging road that could take you back to your starting point). Soon you come to a beautiful, fine-gravel beach beside a deep pool with generally slow-moving water. This is probably the best spot for a picnic, though, depending on the temperament of your charges, you may wish to reserve the stop for the return leg.

9. Almost immediately after this beach, the trail climbs and crosses two pretty little bridges complete with handrails and views upstream to a series of small cascades. The trail goes only a short distance beyond this point, though you can catch an attractive view upstream of another set of rapids and a sharp curve of the river.

10. Although it is possible from here to follow a trail up to the logging roads and back to the trailhead, by far the most attractive option is to return the way you came.

29. STAMP RIVER FALLS VIA STAMP LONG RIVER (ANGLERS') TRAIL/SAYACHLAS T'A SAA'NIM

Two sections of trail, separated by the parking and camping areas of Stamp River Provincial Park. Downstream, the heavily used and more spectacular trails lead a short distance to several views of the dramatic fish ladder, rapids and river gorge. Upstream, the long trail runs through old forest parallel to the deep and fast-flowing river.

LOCATION

Follow Highway 4 to Tofino through North Port Alberni as it descends and comes to a T junction and set of traffic lights. Turn right towards Pacific Rim National Park. Within a short distance cross Kitsuksis Creek bridge, and, almost immediately, turn onto Beaver Creek Road. The signposted entrance to Stamp Falls Provincial Park is about 12.5 km along on the left. Drive to the parking lot. As you begin to descend the hill just before the parking lot, notice a trail on your right entering the forest.

DISTANCE

The short trails downstream total about 2 km. The riverside trail heading upstream is about 15-km return if you walk the whole trail. You can turn back at any point, since there is no distinct destination.

ELEVATION GAIN

100 m, cumulative, over many short sections of switchbacking trail

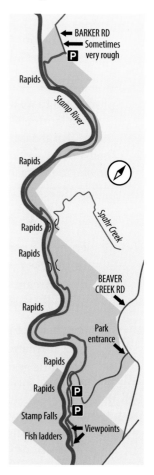

DIFFICULTY

Trail surfaces are generally good, but some of the sections of switchback on the upstream trail can seem steep for small children. Keep in mind, too, that this trail is long for some children.

SEASON

All season, but autumn is best for viewing spawning salmon (and the accompanying happy bears and eagles).

OF SPECIAL INTEREST FOR CHILDREN

An accessible river – and this one is accessible at many points – is always fun for children. The highlight, however, is probably sighting the hordes of spawning salmon thrashing their way up the fish ladder by the falls.

If you plan to walk the trail in one direction and be picked up at the parking lot described in step 5 of the Upstream Section below, be aware that the last short section of the road to this parking area has had a deep washout, preventing all but the sturdiest vehicles from driving to the trailhead.

A. Downstream Section

1. From the parking area, walk along the small road parallel to the river, taking notice of the sign warning against the downstream waterfall if you have small children champing at the bit to jump into the misleadingly placid river.

2. Pass a set of picnic tables with good views over the unusual rock formations clearly visible through the rushing water. Continue gradually upwards until you come to a good viewing promontory, with a chain-linked fence preventing dangerous straying near the cliffs.

3. A little farther along you have a good view of the fish-ladder sections of the surging river. The "falls" (more a series of steep rapids) is farthest away. Closer, inside a twisting

concrete channel, is a series of barricaded and controlled drops for the frantic salmon.

4. Continue along the fenced trail as it climbs to some good views of the deep gorge below the falls. Pause to look at the interpretative signs explaining the different species that, together, provide one of the great salmon-viewing experiences on Vancouver Island.

5. At the split in the trail follow the signs to the viewpoint down the right fork.

6. Along this fenced trail you can look back upstream through the river gorge and, when you come to the turnaround promontory, get an excellent view downstream to a split in the river around an island. A trail, used primarily by fishermen, leads a short distance down this side of the river. However, a much longer trail on the opposite bank runs for some 2 km down the river. Look at the directions in trip 28 (Stamp River – Greenmax Anglers' Trail) to gain access to this beautiful trail.

B. Upstream Section

1. Because of erosion, it is best to retrace the entrance road from your parked car up the slope until you see the trail entering the forest. The trail at first runs along the top of a steep, forested bank before switchbacking down to the banks of the river. The trail runs parallel to the river here, but mostly in the forest under some large cedars, hemlocks and firs. The river is generally slow moving along this section, with some pools and, at one point, a significant bend and side channel.

2. The trail leaves the banks of the river and climbs up switchbacks to run parallel to the river, though set well back from it. Descending another set of switchbacks, the trail crosses a sturdy metal bridge and comes to a substantial, pleasant, gravel beach where the river is deep and fairly swift flowing.

FROM LEFT The view down the gorge, downstream from the fish ladders and falls; one of the favourite picnic spots, slightly upstream from the falls.

3. After leaving the riverbank, the trail once again climbs a series of switchbacks and runs along the top of a high bank before descending again to the river. This pattern, where sections of lower trail switchback to upper trail, is characteristic of much of the route. When, at one high point, you can see a farm field through a thin screen of trees and a sign asking you not to trespass, you know you are nearing the northern end of the trail.

4. Possibly the most interesting part of the trail is the following section, after the trail drops to the riverbank, crosses a large wooden bridge and runs immediately next to the river for about 0.5 km.

5. When the trail starts uphill again, it starts to lead away from the river, and, after passing some particularly large trees, it concludes in a rough gravel parking area where you may have arranged for a pickup. Here there is a sign and map for the whole trail.

6. It is possible to make a loop by turning away from the river at the fork in the trail and returning via the road. However, it is most interesting to return the way you came.

30. KITSUKSIS CREEK

A combination of paved dyke walk, broad gravel trail and an optional, rougher dirt trail along the shores of a creek. The upper part of the trail leads through beautiful forest to a striking view of a small set of falls beneath a trestle, high overhead. The dyke was built after the 1964 earthquake in Alaska that caused tsunami flooding and considerable damage in the area.

LOCATION

Although there are several routes by which you can approach the dyke, one of the easiest is to turn onto the north section of Victoria Quay as it branches off Highway 4 to Tofino just before the Kitsuksis Creek bridge. Park along the side of the road and walk across the Legion parking lot to the corner where the trail starts.

DISTANCE

4.4 km, partial loop

ELEVATION GAIN

30 m

DIFFICULTY

Easy. Children will have to be attended a little at the small falls since the rocks can be slippery and the water can be dangerous when high.

SEASON

All season, but the creek can nearly dry out at the end of a long, hot summer.

OF SPECIAL INTEREST FOR CHILDREN

Children who prefer to cycle while their parents walk will enjoy the paved surface of the dyke for much of the distance and the crushed gravel surface as far as the falls. During spawning season, the sight of coho leaping up the falls beneath the trestle is exciting. As some of your troop will be sure to notice, the lower trail passes two parks with washrooms and playgrounds.

1. Follow the shore of Kitsuksis Creek as the paved dyke curves gently past Blair Park – unless you want to make a visit to any of the facilities there. Since this lowest section of the creek is tidal, you might want to time your visit to coincide with high water, so the creek bed is at its most picturesque – though it is generally screened by small bushes.

2. After passing behind some backyards, most of them well-treed, the dyke trail passes under Gertrude Street bridge and crosses Kitsuksis Creek on a small, purpose-built bridge.

3. Once on the north shore of the creek turn right. Soon you are on a smooth, crushed-gravel surface as the trail winds somewhat away from of the bank of the creek beneath some beautiful large maples and firs. As the trail enters a kind of ravine, thick with sword ferns, it crosses a small wooden bridge and delivers you to a well-positioned viewing spot onto the set of cascading falls and, high overhead, a trestle resting on two huge concrete pillars.

4. Unless you have come on bicycles, continue on the comparatively rough dirt trail. Pass a set of dirt-and-board stairs and a particularly interesting cedar. It is usually hemlock that grow on nurse logs, which, upon rotting away, leave young trees with suspended root systems. In this case, admire the cedar with a strikingly formed double trunk/set of roots.

FROM LEFT The falls beneath the trestle during winter flooding; Small tributary falls near the turn-around spot on the small trail leading upstream from the main falls.

5. A few minutes later, you come to an intriguing set of small falls emerging from the forest opposite and cascading down a shale wall. This makes a reasonably good turnaround spot. The trail continues upstream a little farther but soon leaves the creek and climbs up towards Willow Road.

6. Retrace your route to Gertrude Street bridge. Instead of crossing the small, dyke-trail bridge, go directly ahead to follow the east bank of Kitsuksis Creek.

7. As you approach your starting point, notice a small bridge crossing the creek. Although it is possible to go back to your starting point by taking a paved trail out to Beaver Creek Road and walking along Highway 4 back to Victoria Quay, it is probably most pleasant, instead, to cross Kitsuksis Creek over this bridge to rejoin the dyke trail near your starting point.

31. KITSUKSIS CREEK – MAPLEHURST TRAIL

Loops through some lovely stands of large trees, much of it in Maplehurst Park, descending at points to a charmingly gurgling creek with a "lost world" feeling.

LOCATION
Driving through North Port Alberni towards the highway to Tofino, pass the elementary school on your right and, at a traffic light, turn right onto Gertrude Street. After a little over 1 km, turn right onto Compton Road for 800 m. At the end of Compton Road, turn left onto Willow Road and drive to the end, 750 m along. You have to park on the shoulder of the road, being careful not to block driveways.

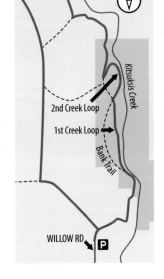

DISTANCE
3.6 km return

ELEVATION GAIN
90 m, descending and rising along a bank

DIFFICULTY
Easy for all but small children who might need help on steeper parts.

SEASON
All season, with boardwalks and small bridges over wetter sections.

OF SPECIAL INTEREST FOR CHILDREN
Small plastic animals and figures have been placed in some nooks of tree trunks and elsewhere. It might be fun to bring along a once-favoured plastic creature and allow your child to

FROM LEFT Even at the end of a dry summer the creek has a few pretty pools; the gentle and restful creek in summer.

give it a new home. At several spots the trail allows easy access to the cheerfully gurgling creek and its pools.

1. Enter the forest at the end of the road, passing the handmade sign for Maplehurst Trail above the first of several small boardwalks and stepping blocks.

2. Continue past views of Kitsuksis Creek far below. Ignore the trail on the left, and, at the next Y junction, past a two-way sign for Bank Trail, turn right at the signposted "1st Creek Loop," pausing to point out the interesting bracket fungus above the sign.

3. Dropping to the creek and crossing a boardwalk, the trail runs close to the water, allowing children to create a little watery havoc. A few large firs and cedars, along with sword ferns and some trees fallen across the creek, give a particularly storybook quality to this part of the creek.

4. Switchback up the bank to join the bank-top trail. After only a few metres, turn right at the sign for 2nd Creek Loop to descend towards the creek again. Notice some especially lovely maidenhair ferns growing around one of the boardwalks by the creek.

A boardwalk through sword ferns on the carefully developed trail system.

5. When the trail again climbs to the top of the bank, turn sharply right to walk along the gradually descending path. Although the creek can't be seen for most of this section, its gurgling is audible through the trees. You soon leave the officially designated park, but the trails continue of the same good quality.

6. Ignore the trail on the left marked with an X and an arrow, and continue ahead for a final visit to the creek before swinging away from the creek and ascending.

7. Once up the bank, you are on a roadbed running more or less straight ahead through smaller trees with many sections of alder and maple. Ignore trails on the left marked with an X and an arrow until you come to a kind of rough T junction.

8. Turn left as the trail swings sharply left, gradually curving back to your right and crossing a small bridge. Pass through a generally open area and rejoin the trail you took on the way out.

32. SCOTT KENNY TRAIL

A new multi-pronged trail in a section of Roger (also called Rogers, Roger's and Rodger's) Creek ravine with two large bridges, fine stands of bigleaf maple and a pretty picnic beach. The trail is named after Port Alberni's former director of Parks, Recreation and Heritage.

LOCATION

At the traffic lights immediately west of the large shopping plazas on the highway entering North Port Alberni, turn south onto Cherry Creek Road (towards Home Hardware). Drive a short distance to the turnaround at the end of the road. There are five trailheads for this trail, since it connects the

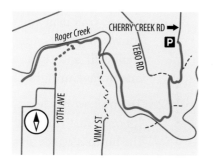

north and south areas of the city (formerly two separate municipalities). The trailhead described here, however, probably makes for the pleasantest and most interesting walk.

DISTANCE

3.6 km

ELEVATION GAIN

40–60 m, cumulative (including optional side trail)

DIFFICULTY

Mostly a broad, smooth trail of crushed gravel, but fairly steep in sections, with a narrow, irregular extension to the main trail.

SEASON

All season, but summer is best for enjoying the stream, and fall is best for viewing the golden blaze of maples and looking for spawning salmon.

OF SPECIAL INTEREST FOR CHILDREN

The little beach at the recommended turnaround spot is great for splashy play. Most of the trail has a good surface for bicycles with sturdy tires, but be aware of the long descent that, on the return leg, becomes a long ascent! Also note that the prettiest part of the trail, the extension to the recommended beach, has a rough, rooty surface.

1. Walk past the large, slickly designed (but somewhat confusing) trail map and enter the largely fir forest. Ignore two converging trails, first one from your left (Broughton Road trailhead) and then, after a nearly 180° curve in the trail, one from your right (Tebo Road trailhead).

2. The trail swings left and begins a long, fairly steep descent. Ignore a dirt trail leading off to the left. When you come to the bottom of the slope, look directly across Roger Creek at one of the shale cliffs that typify creek banks throughout this part of the Alberni Valley. Also notice the new, impressively sturdy bridge crossing the creek. Crossing the creek here would take you up out of the ravine on the other side and into a suburb of South Port Alberni.

3. Don't cross the bridge but turn right. In this section of the flats adjoining the creek there is an astounding concentration of large bigleaf maple. Pass an attractive, deep creek pool, though the opposite bank on this part of the trail is a little bleak from lack of pretty vegetation or trees.

4. Soon come to a second huge and hefty bridge. Cross the bridge and turn right to head downstream, ignoring the trail that leads up to a subdivision. (But note this junction for your return trip.) The trail here is well used, but it is also a little rough in sections. In most places where it has been washed away by the flooding creek, an alternative trail lies to the left.

5. Pass an awkward and ugly bit of the trail, featuring charmless chunks of broken concrete and rusting machinery. Reward

FROM LEFT One of the prettiest parts of the walk is along the rough path just downstream from the official trail; this deep pool makes a great turnaround and picnic spot.

yourself, however, with the lovely climax of your walk – a pretty beach by a deep, green pool at a sharp curve in the creek. Downstream, cliffs dropping straight into the creek make further progress along this side of the creek impossible (though across the creek there are traces of other trails).

6. After soaking in the sights or soaking your feet, turn back until you come to the bridge and the junction with a trail, now on your right, heading up the forested slope. If you have the energy, go at least partway up the climbing trail. From various spots along this ascending trail you have some lovely views into the sword ferns and tall trees at the bottom of the ravine. Since, at the top, the trail fizzles out into an uninspiring subdivision, it is best to turn back when you have absorbed enough view.

7. Retrace your trail across the bridge and back up out of the ravine to your vehicle.

33. CARRIERE ROAD TO SHIP CREEK

A forested route through the extensive network of trails immediately north of the Port Alberni suburbs. Best as one-way trail with shuttle but can be done as a return.

LOCATION

At this writing, the Carriere Road trailhead is unsignposted but easy to find. Drive into Port Alberni on the Port Alberni Highway, noticing where it changes name to Redford Street. From the major intersection of Redford Street with 10th Avenue (by a shopping plaza and traffic lights), head south (towards Save-On Foods) on 10th Avenue two blocks to Burde Street. Turn left. Follow Burde Street for 2.3 km until you see Carriere Road on your right. (Shortly before Carriere Road take note of the signposted trailheads on either side of Burde Street for other sections of the trail system.) Park at the end of the road in a large gravel turnaround.

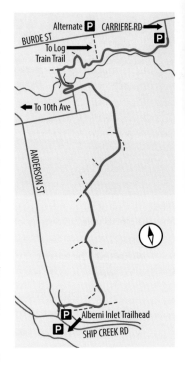

If you have two cars, you may want to leave one at the far end of the route to allow a one-way walk. If so, instead of turning onto Burde Street, keep ahead on 10th Avenue for 1.2 km, until you reach Argyle Street. Turn left and taken the fourth street on your right, Anderson Street. Drive almost to the end of Anderson Street, keeping your eye out for the signposted Ship Creek Trailhead, about 100 m before the T junction with Franklin River Road.

DISTANCE

5.7 km, one-way

Three bridges in a row near the beginning of the route.

ELEVATION GAIN
130 m, net (with starting and end points at same elevation)

DIFFICULTY
Easy, crushed-gravel surface and/or old roadbed, but the overall length and elevation change might be problematic for small children.

SEASON
All season

OF SPECIAL INTEREST FOR CHILDREN
This is one of the best trails in Port Alberni for kids with mountain bikes, though only those used to handling hills will feel comfortable. If Mum and Pop are up to it, this could be a great cycling venture for the whole family. Walking, however, is clearly an option.

1. Take the trail entering the forest immediately to the left of the fire hydrant. Once on the trail, there are signs for Log Train Trail and "Estevan," both pointing to the right. Both of these destinations lie off your route, but, for now, go towards them. The first section of this trail is probably the

prettiest part of the whole route. Some large hemlocks and maples with a thick undergrowth of sword ferns shade the winding trail. Cross three pretty bridges in a row. A deep ravine slopes off to your left for a section until the trail swings away towards a subdivision.

2. Pass immediately behind some houses through a growth of small trees. Children on bicycles might find a little daunting the fairly steep but short downhill. When you come to a junction with a trail to Log Train Trail, leading to your right, go straight ahead towards "Estevan" (a trailhead lying slightly off your route). Ignore a broad trail from your right merging with the route straight ahead. When you come to two signs, both pointing left, one to "Argyle" and the other to "Ship Ck," turn left. (Ship Creek is your destination.)

3. Follow the very broad trail downhill and cross an unusual, steel footbridge high above a creek (usually nearly dry by the end of a long summer). Look for the lovely patch of maiden hair fern on the steep rocks opposite. Climb gradually up through sword ferns and maples to emerge behind a subdivision.

4. A sign indicating the way to "Ship Ck" and "Comox St" will point you in the right direction behind these houses. At the end of the row of houses, the trail takes a sharp turn to the right (to skirt the houses) before entering a stand of second-growth fir. At this point the trail is largely an old roadbed, perfect for easy mountain biking.

5. Ignore the sign directing you to China Creek on your right. Pass a semicircular set of benches on your left and ignore the broad trail beside it. You soon come to two signs, one pointing back to "Argyle" and, through the trees a short distance, to "15th Ave." Ignore these and spot, on the opposite side of the trail, the sign for Ship Creek, pointing to a sharp turn left.

6. The broad dirt trail climbs consistently but gradually for a considerable distance before levelling out. Ignore the sign to the right for "Comox St." A separate sign saying simply

An unusual footbridge over the fern-lined gorge.

"Trail" and pointing in both directions reassures you that you are, indeed, on the right track! Pass a trail on the left and drop down a steep hill, another bit of a challenge for any wobbly cyclists in your group.

7. A sign will point you on your way to Ship Creek, but, immediately afterwards, come to an unsignposted split in the trail. While these routes rejoin, take the right fork to circle back, and, at the T junction, take a sharp left to take a swooping trail downhill to a major trailhead. Those who have also hiked along the Alberni Inlet Trail, or wish to make an epic venture, will be interested to see that the trailhead for this (now a 24-km set of trails) is clearly visible a short distance down the road to the left.

8. The large parking area to the left of the trailhead is a good place to have left a shuttle vehicle. Otherwise return to the point where you started, either by retracing your route or, if you prefer, making your way through the city streets.

34. ROGER CREEK & BEAR DEN TRAIL LOOP

A heavily forested creekside trail passing historic remains of a dam, three interesting bridges and a characteristic sequence of shale cliffs and pools.

Various versions of the creek's name, Roger (Rogers, Roger's, Rodger's), appear on maps and signs. Locals traditionally use the first, though the second is more correct since the creek purportedly takes its name from the same Colonel Rogers who mapped Rogers Pass.

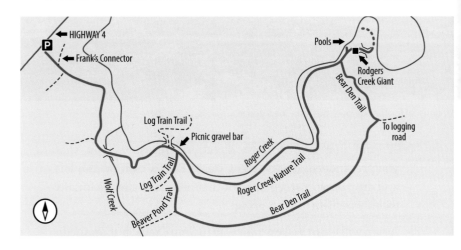

LOCATION
If you are entering the Alberni Valley from the Parksville direction, drive 1.5 km past the Tourist Information Centre on the Port Alberni Highway. On your left is a gravel parking area for several cars and a carved wooden sign saying "Rogers Creek Nature Trail."

DISTANCE
4.8 km, partial loop, partial repeat

ELEVATION GAIN
Approximately 200 m, cumulative, with many ups and downs

Slate cliffs and clear emerald pools near the end of the trail.

DIFFICULTY
Moderately tiring for younger children, but generally easy to walk, with a few rooty sections.

SEASON
All season but can be muddy in sections. Early summer is perhaps best for water play, since the creek shrinks mostly to a few pools at the end of a dry summer.

OF SPECIAL INTEREST FOR CHILDREN
Access to the creek, especially by some pools, two high bridges to explore, and the "Rodger's Creek Giant" (complete with interpretative sign) to admire.

1. Take a quick look at the large, slick map at the trailhead, but don't study it too carefully – it can mislead you about trail names and routes. Start down the broad, easy trail, passing the sign for Frank's Connector on your left and a few

minutes later, a strange little sign for Gen's Trails nestled in a mossy maple. Very shortly afterwards come to signposted Wolf Creek and a particularly pretty bridge over the (usually) tiny creek.

2. The trail soon provides you with views of Roger Creek down a wooded slope but then swings away from the creek. When you come to a split in the trail, take the right fork to dip around a small ravine (and seasonal creek), though notice that many walkers have made a fairly steep shortcut directly across the ravine.

3. In a few minutes, arrive at a broad gravel bar on the banks of Roger Creek and the concrete remains of a small dam, historically used to collect water for Port Alberni. Unless the creek is in flood, you can cross the bar to an islet and a picnic table framed by a charming, arched sign announcing your arrival at the "Bavarian Beer Garden"! Don't get your hopes up: you must provide your own beer and bratwurst. Here also is the new, sturdy footbridge high above the creek and forming part of Log Train Trail (see the next trip, 35, for this trail).

4. Turning back up from the creek bank notice a dizzying array of signs. Follow the one saying "Canyon Roger Ck Tr," leading along the south shore of the creek. This next section of the trail allows you many good views of the creek and some interesting features, including a shale-ridge creek bed at one point, and, at others, deep pools beneath shale cliffs. After a deep curve in the creek, the trail allows access to the creek side and, of interest in hot weather, some lovely pools.

5. The next section of the trail is sometimes a little overgrown, but it is fairly short. When you come to the "Bear Den Trail" post, note the junction for your return trip. For now, however, continue straight head for the easiest access to gravel beaches and pools.

6. After visiting these pools, return to the trail to go the short distance to "Rodger's Creek Giant." Along with other

FROM LEFT A carefully crafted rustic bridge near "Rodger's Creek Giant"; an accessible spot for splashing and wading.

interesting facts, a sign points out that the tree is a remarkable 66 m tall, only slightly shorter than the tallest Douglas fir in Cathedral Grove. Almost immediately you come to a pretty rustic bridge and a stone set of steps leading to a ridgetop section of trail. You may wish to make this your turn-back spot. At this writing, the loop trail indicated on the trailhead map is largely overgrown. This small trail does lead to a beach, another reasonable turnaround spot, but it doesn't form a clear loop as the map suggests. In either case, return to the Bear Den Trail junction.

7. Turn up Bear Den Trail, climbing slowly but considerably through comparatively small firs and maples above a bed of sword fern. At a signposted junction, one direction indicating "To Logging Road" (not shown on the trailhead map), turn right to stay on Bear Den Trail.

8. Follow this easy, high trail to the signposted junction with Beaver Pond Trail, and turn right. Follow Beaver Pond Trail a short distance to a T junction with Log Train Trail. Turn right onto this trail to descend a long slope to the multi-signed junction with the Roger Creek main trail. Turn left and return to the trailhead.

35. BEAVER POND & LOG TRAIN TRAIL LOOP

*A combination of trails within the extensive network of trails
around Roger (also called Rogers, Roger's and Rodger's) Creek
near Port Alberni, featuring a dramatic bridge crossing
of Roger Creek, and a pretty little lake with good views
of a beaver lodge.*

LOCATION
Maebelle Road forms a T junction with the Port Alberni Highway about 500 m west of the junction signposted for Bamfield to the left and Tofino to the right. Turn left towards Bamfield on the Port Alberni Highway and park along the side of Maebelle Road near the Port Alberni Highway. Notice a large wooden sign saying "Access to Log Train Trail" across the highway.

DISTANCE
5.2 km, mostly loop

ELEVATION GAIN
80 m, cumulative, spread over two gradual climbs

DIFFICULTY
Generally easy, though sometimes rooty, dirt trails, with one fairly steep, switchbacking drop. Optional return route has a steep dirt slope for a few metres.

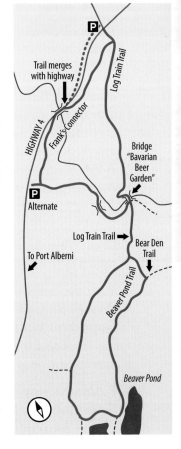

SEASON
All season, though Roger Creek can lose most of its running water at the end of a long summer (while keeping some pretty pools).

A beaver lodge is clearly visible near the islet in the middle of the large pond.

OF SPECIAL INTEREST FOR CHILDREN

The name "Beaver Pond" says it all – though, admittedly, the chances of seeing Bucky the Beaver aren't high. The newly constructed bridge over Roger Creek is an additional feature for children who like to drop twigs into the flowing stream. The picnic table and gravel bar below the bridge are a good rest stop and opportunity to get miserably wet feet.

1. Cross the highway with caution and enjoy the easy stroll through a pleasant Douglas fir and salal forest, ignoring a smaller trail leading off to the right. This is Frank's Connector, which you may use to complete the loop hike.

2. A direct and largely level walk through the forest will soon bring you to the top of a steep bank. From this point the trail descends over several switchbacks to a newly constructed, impressive footbridge high over Roger Creek. Handrails both on the switchbacks and on the bridge make this steepest and potentially most challenging part of the route easy and secure.

3. Cross the bridge and drop down onto a kind of treed island in the middle of Roger Creek. In fact, it is only during floods that this becomes a proper island. With its picnic table and hand-carved sign announcing the picnic spot to be the "Bavarian Beer Garden," this is an inviting rest spot. Here there are chunks of concrete, evidence of the construction that once made this a reservoir.

4. Once on the riverbank, you are confronted by a bewildering number of signs. Ignoring the trails to the right and to the left, go more or less straight ahead towards Log Train Trail. Climb the long, sloping trail through sword ferns and fairly large, second-growth firs. When you come to a signposted trail leading sharply to your left onto Beaver Pond Trail, veer left and proceed until you come to a T junction.

5. Turn right, ignoring Bear Den Trail leading in from the left. From here to Beaver Pond the trail is direct and clear. When you come to the little lake you find two or three spots where you can get a good view of the beaver lodge across the water.

6. Partway along the shore of the lake, turn away and, heading downhill, traverse around the shores of another pond barely visible to your left. As you leave this second pond behind you, turn right to begin the return leg of your trip. The comparatively narrow trail will bring you to a kind of crossroads with signposted Log Train Trail. Turn right to follow Log Train Trail back to the creek.

7. Once at the creek, and the junction with multiple signs, turn left to follow the creek downstream to the main trailhead.

FROM LEFT The large new bridge over Roger Creek; a close-up of the beaver lodge.

Much of this part of the trail is a little back from the creek and above it, but you can catch glimpses of water through the trees. When you get to a small ravine, note the fairly steep shortcut across it, but the main trail circles to your left around the dip. Shortly before the end of the trail cross a pretty little bridge over Wolf Creek.

8. When you get within spitting distance of the main trailhead of the Roger Creek trail network, follow the sign for Frank's Connector on your right. Turn right and follow it, roughly parallel to the highway until it brings you out to the highway. At this point use the main highway bridge to cross Roger Creek.

9. Once across the creek, angling off to your right, the continuation of the connector leads up a steep dirt bank. The operative word is "steep." Getting up this bank, especially when the slope is dry and slippery, can be a bit of a struggle. Once up the bank, however, the narrow trail winds easily through salal to join Log Train Trail near its beginning. If you decide clambering up the steep bit isn't for you, walk the short distance beside the highway back to the trailhead.

36. HOLE IN THE WALL

A short walk to some of the most strikingly unusual configurations of rock and water on Vancouver Island.

LOCATION
At the end of Highway 4's descent into the Alberni Valley, slow down when you see Coombs Country Candy ahead on your right and, a short distance before it on your left, a wide but unsign-posted gravel shoulder, usually hosting at least one parked car.

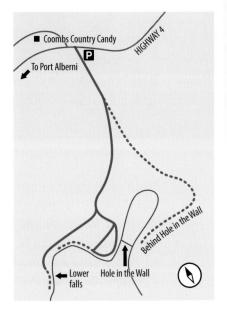

DISTANCE
1.7-km return, with a partial loop and longer option

ELEVATION GAIN
60 m

DIFFICULTY
Mostly easy to the first falls, the so-called Hole in the Wall. The route to the best view of the second falls can be a little tricky just before the falls.

SEASON
All season, but walking down the creek bed towards the lower falls is best when the water level is fairly low, usually in summer. If the winter flood waters are high, they can wash away the rock sculptures.

OF SPECIAL INTEREST FOR CHILDREN
The waterfall pouring out of a giant hole is a wonderful sight, but so, too, are the literally hundreds of stacked-rock creations partway down the creek towards the second falls (unless they've

been washed away by winter floods). Some children may want to try their hand at creating their own and add to the collection. Wading down the creek in summer is easy, comfortable and great fun.

1. The trail is unmistakeable at the beginning, both because it is wide and easy and because some kind soul has handcrafted a wooden sign announcing "Hole in the Wall." Within a very short distance, come to a large open area and a branch in the track. Note the track straight ahead across the open area, since this is the beginning of an optional route to the other side of Hole in the Wall.

2. Take the right branch indicated by a second directional sign, though you might not see this sign at first. Go straight ahead, ignoring another, smaller branch to the right. The broad, gravel roadbed through a clear-cut area descends quite quickly to some forest ahead and another split.

3. Take the left branch into the forest, again indicated by a directional sign, though note the other branch for later exploration. Descend this broad dirt trail (sometimes eroded and rough) as it makes a wide C curve and brings you to a well-trodden flat area underneath some beautiful, large cedars and firs. Straight ahead is the wonderful little stepped falls emerging from aptly named Hole in the Wall. Though you may want to maintain the sense of wonder and mystery by not chirping up with an explanation, the slightly dreary fact is that the hole was chopped through an unusual shale wall (created by a sharp bend in the creek) and served as part of the original system that once provided water to Port Alberni.

4. After lingering by these falls for slightly too long, follow the shore of the creek downstream until, after a short distance you come to an amazing display of stacked-rock sculptures, some of them reminiscent of inuksuks.

CLOCKWISE FROM ABOVE LEFT The strange Hole in the Wall has a relatively pedestrian history: helping provide water to Port Alberni; downstream from Hole in the Wall, many wonderful rock castles pop up each summer – only to be washed away each winter; the swimming pool at the bottom of the lower falls.

5. From here you can carry on down the creek to the second falls, much higher and especially lovely because of the clear pool at the base. You can walk along the edge of the creek for part of the distance towards these falls but doing so means wading through a pebbly section just before the falls. Do be aware, however, if you come to the falls this way you must undertake a precipitous and potentially dangerous section of scrambling to get to a good view spot for the lower falls. It is best to retrace your route upstream until you see a trail headed off away from the shore, though a fallen tree at the beginning of this otherwise good trail can obscure it slightly. Rejoin the main route to Hole in the Wall.

6. Climb the trail to the junction at the top of the bank, largely out of the trees.

7. Turn left and follow this bank-top track downstream. Ignore two tracks to your right. Soon you hear the rush from the lower falls through the trees and see the beginning of a smaller trail dropping towards the creek. A trail has been dug into the loose shale slope and thoughtfully provided with a rope, thus allowing a moderately secure descent to the best viewing area for the lower falls. Depending on conditions and the nimbleness of your companions, however, you may reasonably opt not to test your luck.

8. Return to the large open area near the highway trailhead.

Optional Add-On: Behind Hole in the Wall

For an additional 1-km out and back, you can take the wide track/ roadbed leading from the large open area near the trailhead to the right and proceeding downhill. This route descends and curves to the right to bring you to an excellent view spot for the back of Hole in the Wall. Some adventurous spirits during summer low-water clamber through the hole.

37. ALBERNI LOOKOUT

One of the oldest and most-beloved trails in the Alberni Valley, climbing to a rocky bluff, once the site of a forestry lookout tower. Magnificent views over the entire valley. This trail is not in parkland but runs through Island Timberlands forest. Be prepared to respect any signposted closures.

LOCATION
The clearest landmark is Coombs Country Candy at the entrance to the Alberni Valley along the Alberni Highway (4) just under 1 km east of the Visitor Centre. Just uphill from the store, turn onto Lacy Lake Road and park in the gravel area on the side of the road.

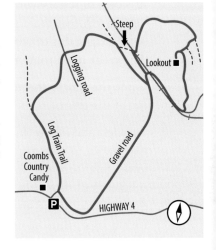

DISTANCE
4.5-km loop

ELEVATION GAIN
280 m

DIFFICULTY
Moderate, though tiring for little legs. The trail is safe but fairly rough underfoot at spots and steep at places. At one short section, care should be taken under dry conditions as it is easy to slide on the loose dirt and pebbles. Small children should be minded from going too close to the cliffs immediately below the lookout spot, since there are no guardrails or fences.

SEASON
All season, but during the wettest weather some sections of the trail can turn into minor stream beds!

The whole area around the historic lookout is open bluffs.

OF SPECIAL INTEREST FOR CHILDREN

Besides the exhilarating view from the steep-sided bluff, probably most interesting for children – in autumn – might be the wild apple tree at the side of the railway tracks. (Though this also can be a favourite haunt of a local, apple-loving bear!)

1. Start uphill and turn left onto broad Log Train Trail (this trail extends many kilometres up the valley).

2. In a few minutes, turn onto a broad, dirt-and-rock trail leading uphill. This trail, like many in the area, has been used by mountain bikers, though many sections are so washed out

and rough that you can expect to see few intrepid cyclists. After climbing, the trail crosses a recently used logging road and passes a newly logged area clearly visible to the left.

3. Climb this trail past some washed-out sections, over boulders and roots, until you come to an old roadbed cutting across the trail. It is possible to make a shortcut by going straight ahead up this trail, but this section of the trail is rough and very steep. Instead of attempting this route, turn right along the largely horizontal roadbed.

4. In a short distance, reach a T junction with a larger gravel road (you come down this road on the return leg of the loop). Turn left and head gradually uphill until you come to the railway tracks.

5. Instead of going all the way to the tracks, turn left onto a dirt track running parallel to the railway tracks. This route goes a short distance before approaching the tracks.

6. Cross the tracks and climb a narrow but clear trail up the bank. Probably the most attractive part of the route, this trail climbs while traversing a slope that drops off to the left to a kind of gully with sword ferns and moderately large firs.

7. As you approach the lookout summit, you can see below you on the left a dirt road (used primarily by ATVs). This whole summit area is criss-crossed with many different paths and routes, but you can navigate these by selecting the trail that most leads upwards. Almost immediately this strategy involves your taking a fairly small but clear trail forking uphill to your right.

8. When you reach the open bluff, the site of the former forest-fire lookout, you can wander at will over the various bluffs and knolls, looking for the best views. Prominent amongst the various landmarks that spread out in front of you are the Alberni Inlet ("the canal" to locals), Sproat Lake

The view across the valley to distant Sproat Lake and the iconic Mt. Klitsa.

and the most iconic of local landmarks, Mt. Klitsa, usually well supplied with snow throughout most of the summer.

9. Although you see many different broad tracks leading away from the bluffs, the comparatively narrow trail downhill begins immediately behind the bluffs, running roughly parallel to the cliffs below the bluffs. When you come across a split as it passes a fairly awkward area, opt for the left fork, though both branches of the trail rejoin. Immediately before the trail reaches a gravel road, it can be slippery in dry weather with loose dirt and pebbles. Now be grateful that you wore shoes with a good grip!

10. Once on the gravel road, follow it right to run parallel to the railway tracks. Just before it crosses the tracks you see a venerable volunteer apple tree, and, if you are lucky, you can find a little snack (while not taking more than your fair share).

11. Follow this broad, gravel road on an easy, direct descent to your vehicle.

38. WESLEY RIDGE

*A fairly steep ascent through Douglas firs and arbutus
to breathtaking views of Cameron Lake. An optional extension
along a generally much-easier trail leads to a high point
and views along the east coast of the island.*

LOCATION

When driving on Highway 4 from Parksville,
look for the Little Qualicum Falls Provincial
Park sign on your right, and start measuring. After 3.8 km, just after crossing the
bridge for Lockwood Creek, pull over into
a prominent gravel parking area next to
railway tracks. If you are coming from Port
Alberni, this spot is about 1 km past the east
end of Cameron Lake.

DISTANCE

4.8-km return

ELEVATION GAIN

510 m

DIFFICULTY

This is probably the most challenging hike
in this book. The trail is often quite steep
and rocky, and the climb is considerable
for young 'uns. Near the beginning of the
trail there is a rocky section provided with
a rope. If your family is comfortable on this
part, they will be comfortable with the steepest parts on the
rest of the trail. If not, a good alternative is to drive less than
1 km in the direction of Cameron Lake to the signposted trail
for Mt. Cokely. See *Popular Day Hikes 4 Vancouver Island* for a
description of this trail.

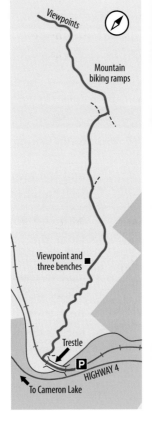

SEASON

Depending on conditions, all season. At nearly 700 m, the upper part of the ridge can often have snow in winter. You can check snow conditions by looking at the ridge from the highway around Cameron Lake. Also, take care crossing the rocky sections in icy conditions.

OF SPECIAL INTEREST FOR CHILDREN

This is the kind of hike, with its bits of scrambling and sense of height, that can bring out the fledgling mountaineering spirit – at least if you're lucky.

Some general advice on keeping to the best trail, particularly when coming down. Always choose the route that is most heavily travelled, even though it may look steeper than a smaller side route. At a few points, these "false friends" start out gently enough but soon turn on you. Be advised.

---

1. Start out towards Cameron Lake along the railway tracks, crossing over a trestle within a few minutes. About 200 m from the parking area, look for a well-used trail on the right, dipping into the salal.

2. Ignore a small trail to the right leading down towards the creek. The trail ahead wastes no time in giving you a taste of what lies ahead. Almost immediately, start to climb. Because the trail is user-made, all the switchbacks on the route are short and fairly steep. The forest is almost entirely of older Douglas firs, none of them huge because of the difficult growing conditions on the dry, steep slope.

3. In slightly more than five minutes, arrive at almost the steepest sections of the whole trail. Some kind soul has put in place a bit of rope, though it is best not to lean back on the rope. Instead, use it only for any additional security your family might want.

4. The trail varies in steepness, but generally zigzags up the spine of the ridge. After climbing about 200 m vertical, come to a fairly steep opening in the trees. This spot provides you with your first glimpses of a distant view, as well as your first encounters with the charming little manzanita bushes that dot the higher, exposed slopes. The trail splits at few spots across this open section, but the branch trails converge.

5. After ascending about 250 m, you get your first peeks of Cameron Lake and the beginning of an especially beautiful area, looking for all the world like a (rather steep) rock garden of manzanita, arbutus and moss. In fact, within a few scrambling steps, you are at a magnificent viewing spot – the first of three benches perched along the slope. Each of these has its own style, character and view. The one carved with the words "Forever Tuesday" may provoke the most smiles!

6. For many visitors, and possibly your family, this is the best destination and, fittingly, a good picnic spot. Others may wish to continue to the high point.

Optional Add-On: Route to the High Point
By the time you reach the viewing area with three benches you have only gained half the elevation of the highest point on this route. Still, the trail from here on up is almost entirely gentle – and, therefore, covers a lot more distance.

1. Leaving the benches view spot, the trail enters forest and almost immediately levels out considerably. After ambling through small firs, come to a puzzling fork – puzzling because both the main trail swinging left and the fork on the right (usually blocked by branches) might just resemble a disused ATV track. In fact, that is precisely what it is. Dismayingly, the comparatively gentle slopes on the north side of Wesley Ridge are interlaced with ATV tracks, some of them impinging on the walking trail.

CLOCKWISE FROM ABOVE The first of three benches with views down Cameron Lake; from near the radio tower, a view to the southeast; Mt. Arrowsmith towers above Wesley Ridge.

2. Go left (actually, straight ahead). Soon the track narrows to become a lovely trail, entering a kind of gentle declivity of forest with little undergrowth and a high canopy. Dropping slightly, cross this dip and come to a significant split. The trail to the left is usually marked with several chunks of flagging tape. This is the route that leads to a traverse of the whole length of Wesley Ridge. A much closer and more immediately gratifying destination with great views lies along the route to the right. A short distance up this ATV track brings you to a T junction. Turn left.

3. This next section takes you on an eye-popping tour of a decaying sequence of amazingly scary wooden structures designed for daredevil mountain bikers. As the slope steepens, the path narrows and becomes more challenging. One short bit is as steep as anything you've encountered so far on Wesley Ridge. It does, however, bring you to expansive rock bluffs and the first of many stunning views of Vancouver Island's east coast.

4. The views only get better as you make your way through the open, mossy bluffs towards the transmitter tower at the high point. In your fascination with trying to locate your great-aunt's house far below, don't forget to swivel in the opposite direction for some equally impressive views of Mt. Cokely and Mt. Arrowsmith.

5. Return the way you came, preparing yourself to take more care going down those steep sections than you probably felt necessary when coming up.

39. LITTLE QUALICUM FALLS PROVINCIAL PARK

*A full-facility park in old-growth forest, with trails
and bridges over a deep gorge with several sets of falls.*

LOCATION

The park is 20 km from Parksville
on Highway 4 towards Port Alberni,
clearly signposted with a wooden
provincial parks sign. Drive past the
first, small parking lot on your left
and park in the second, larger parking lot by a picnic shelter and washroom facility.

DISTANCE

2-km loop (a kind of figure eight)

ELEVATION GAIN

80 m, cumulative

DIFFICULTY

Easy, broad park path but with a
fairly steep set of steps that the
smallest children might need help
with. Potentially dangerous bridges
and cliffs are – in most places – well
fenced off.

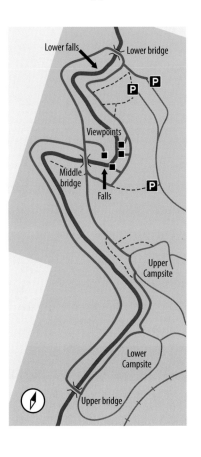

SEASON

All season, since even in a dry summer the falls are dramatic.

OF SPECIAL INTEREST FOR CHILDREN

The high bridges, deep gorges and dangerously plunging cliffs
will capture the imagination of most children. Because of fatal
accidents, swimming is forbidden along the river starting at a
point 75 m above the middle bridge.

The gorge just below the upper falls makes for one of the best viewing spots.

1. Take the path from the end of the parking lot, with the washrooms to your left. Both in this area and along the trail, take time to appreciate some of the magnificent, old-growth Douglas firs. As you descend the bank, pass the first path on your left and continue to the path closest to the river. At this point you are slightly above the lower, smaller falls.

2. Turn left to follow the track upstream, staying closest to the river gorge, but being careful not to stray from the trail. Ignore two trails approaching from the left. As you follow

the river upstream, round a sharp bend and look ahead to one of the most impressive sights of this area. Though the view of the upper falls is a little obscured, viewing the rushing water from this vantage point provides a powerful sense of the height and steepness of the cliffs and the power of the water. Three separate viewpoints along this section allow *Ooh* and *Ahh* perspectives on this magnificent bit of the gorge.

3. As you ascend, look across the gorge to the fenced viewing area to absorb the scale of the scenery. The climbing trail joins a broad trail from the left and brings you to the middle bridge over the river. At this point you are upstream from the famous double falls.

4. Cross the bridge, for now postponing the thrill of visiting these falls. Instead, turn left to follow a broad, gravel track upstream, though soon it becomes narrow and rooty. Mostly close to the river, the trail allows pretty views of the rapidly rushing water over boulders and past small pools. The forest of large, but not huge, cedar and Douglas fir gives way to smaller trees as you approach the upper bridge.

5. Cross the gently arched wooden bridge to find yourself in the Lower Campground. Turn left onto the gravel campground road, passing several tent sites on either side of the road. At the end of the loop, a fairly broad, gravel trail descends towards the river. While it may seem to reach a dead end at the riverbank, in fact it goes to the right of a large cedar and, after crossing a wet spot, leads to an attractive, well-structured riverside section, slightly above the shore itself.

6. After a short distance, the trail splits. Unfortunately, the riverside section is closed (as is indicated by a prominent yellow sign), so you must take the right fork and climb a few stone steps up to the Upper Campground. Just a few steps along the gravel campground road, however, opposite Site 31, you can turn down another trail.

FROM LEFT There is nothing little about the falls in winter; the summer version of the falls.

7. Ignore two trails leading off to the right and carry on more or less parallel to the river, but increasingly distant from it. When you come to the middle bridge, cross it again and turn right. The geography can be a little confusing here because the main loop trail is to the left, leading well away from the river. To view the falls from their most spectacular angles, follow the wooden sign pointing the way to the "Viewpoint." This entire area is well-protected by chain-link fence, of course, but a little puzzling at first is the fact that you have to walk through a fenced corridor along a steep-sided ridge.

8. Return to the main trail as it swings away from the river gorge and drops below the level of the lower falls. These falls, though farther away from the best viewing spot (the centre of the bridge), have a different character from the upper falls as they squeeze between wedges of rock. The bare, convoluted rock along the channel makes vividly clear how high flood waters have sculpted the cliffs.

9. Once across the bridge, rejoin your original trail and climb back up to the parking lot.

40. ENGLISHMAN RIVER FALLS PROVINCIAL PARK

*Deservedly one of the most popular parks on the island,
with good trails past magnificent old Douglas firs, spectacular
river gorges and, of course, impressive falls.*

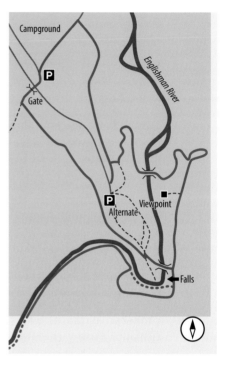

LOCATION
From Highway 4 out of Parksville, drive for about 13 km and turn at the well-signposted corner of Errington Road. The park is located at the end of the road a little under 9 km along.

DISTANCE
4.2-km loop (shorter options)

ELEVATION GAIN
30 m

DIFFICULTY
Easy park trail with a good surface, but a little rooty in some spots.

SEASON
All season, since falls are good even in a dry summer, though at their most spectacular during winter and spring.

OF SPECIAL INTEREST FOR CHILDREN
The thunder of the falls viewed from a dizzyingly high bridge is the obvious attraction, but some children will be impressed by the size of some of the old firs and, at points, the possibility of getting wet.

1. Don't drive all the way to the main parking lot but instead turn left into a small parking area at the entrance to the

camping area. Check out the outhouses and a large directional map posted. Head left to walk into the campground, passing several tent sites. When you come to a wooden sign indicating "Lower Falls," turn right to begin the truly beautiful part of your walk.

2. The trail runs roughly parallel to the river gorge on your left through some inspiring old-growth firs. It maintains elevation until it almost runs next to the road on the right, at which point it begins to descend. After a short distance you come to some concrete steps bringing you to a T junction with a broad, crushed-gravel trail.

3. Turn left to descend along the wide switchbacks through the heavily forested slope. The final switchback brings you downstream from the bridge over the lower falls, so you can approach these falls behind the protection of a chain-link fence. Turn onto the bridge to gape at the views of the stunningly high cliffs upstream, and, downstream, the deep pools – in warm weather with a few occupants! Unfortunately, the lower falls have lost much of their drop since the collapse of a huge chunk of rock, but the view upstream remains impressive.

4. Once across the bridge, the trail rises and swings downstream, passing the steep dirt track that is occasionally used by those clambering to the pools you saw from the bridge. Climb some stone stairs, and zigzag back to begin the upstream section of your walk. Don't ignore the viewpoint on your right for the vertiginous view it gives you of the plummet down the vertical sides of the gorge into the swirling waters.

5. When you get to the bridge for the upper falls, continue straight ahead. Initially, this trail gives intriguing side views onto the falls but then crosses over a small bridge and leads upstream inland for a section, before emerging on the riverbank well above the falls. And voila! Just when you least

Although the lower falls have largely disappeared because of rockfall, the gorge itself is impressive.

expected it – an outhouse. But it's there for a good reason: this is a popular gathering spot where the water splashes and swirls around the boulders on its way to the falls. The dangers of going far into the water here – above the falls – hardly need spelling out.

6. The trail continues upstream until you come to a sign marking the park boundary and announcing that you should not go farther. The size of the trail suggests, accurately, that many continue beyond the park boundary. (In case you're wondering, the trail does continue for almost another kilometre, with side trails down to some gorgeous, deep pools and gravel beaches, before turning away from the river and climbing up to a clear-cut area.)

CLOCKWISE FROM LEFT The lower falls in winter; even in summer the falls are impressive for the way they drop into an angled crevice; the falls in winter thunder impressively.

7. Turning back towards the upper bridge, notice a small, unofficial trail running by the bank. This trail is passable, but it does require a bit of scrambling across damp areas and up over some steep roots before it rejoins the proper trail.

8. After drinking in the view of the unusually angled falls plunging into a deep cleft, cross the bridge and take the trail to the left up to a small knoll. Continue along this trail, with good views onto the river, until it enters the forest. From here back to your vehicle, the track is actually a service road that passes some clusters of magnificent old trees. At a T junction, turn right to go the short distance past a yellow gate, and, across the paved road, to your parked vehicle.

41. MORRISON CREEK FALLS

A favourite with a small group of local enthusiasts, this pretty waterfall, with its unusually smooth lip, is approached easily and framed beautifully by large, overhanging cedars.

LOCATION
Driving along Highway 4 towards Port Alberni from Parksville, turn down Errington Road, prominently signposted for Englishman River Provincial Park. When you reach the Gas N Go at the central intersection in Errington, start measuring with your odometer. After 4.7 km along Errington Road, turn left onto Dobson Road and drive for 1.3 km. Make a left turn onto Fairdowne Road, and, after 300 m, turn right onto Stagdowne Road. At the end of the road, park in a broad, circular turnaround.

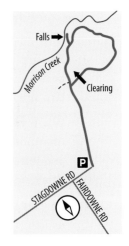

DISTANCE
2 km

ELEVATION GAIN
15 m, cumulative

DIFFICULTY
Generally easy grade, but the trail near the falls is fairly narrow and can be slippery when wet. The descent of a small gully to the base of the falls is not dangerous, but it can be awkward in wet weather. A length of rope has been put in place to minimize the chances of a painful fall. The return route, sometimes a little bushy, is well-trod, partially by horses.

SEASON
All season, except during a dry summer when the creek shrinks drastically.

OF SPECIAL INTEREST FOR CHILDREN

Most children, like most people, are intrigued by waterfalls. Unlike some of the most spectacular falls nearby, these falls can be viewed from their base without risking life and limb.

Because the walk is not in a park, be sure to respect any signs forbidding entry, should they appear.

---

1. The first part of the walk is an easy tromp down an old road-bed, level and mostly clear, chiefly through small firs. Ignore two side trails on your left (used by horses).

2. When you get to an open area, notice three narrower trails, one more or less straight ahead, the others to your right and left, respectively. The loop trail to the falls concludes at this junction.

3. To visit the falls, enter the forest on the straight-ahead trail, usually marked with orange flagging tape, surrounded by sword ferns, salal and second-growth but fairly mature Douglas firs. Some logs have fallen across the trail but are small enough to step over easily. Partway to the falls, the trail dips for a short section and may be a little soggy in wet weather. A little light-footedness could be handy. Look for occasional, reassuring (but unnecessary) bits of flagging tape.

4. At this writing, two small trees are lying across the entrance to the side trail to the falls on your left. A piece of flagging tape, and the clearly visible trail, should get you on your way after a little clambering. Soon after you hear the sound of rushing water, you can view the falls from a few metres behind and above. From here the trail angles down the bank, bringing you to a much more direct view spot. With a little persistence, it is possible to get a good view of the falls, beautifully framed by some large cedars.

CLOCKWISE FROM LEFT Large cedars and the crisp edge of the falls create a distinctive sights; the unusual brown of the water occurs only during flood conditions; the view of the falls from the trail above the main drop.

5. Climb back up from the falls and turn left along the trail. A little bushy at some points, particularly from encroaching salal, the trail is level, well-used and clear. At first the creek is visible down the bank to your left, but the trail soon leads into the trees away from the creek into a stand of some of the most beautiful, large fir in the area. Keep your eyes open for some particularly interesting specimens, one unusually forked. As the trail swings right and moves into an area mostly of large alder and smaller maple, you know you are nearing the end of the loop. Within minutes, walk into the clearing to rejoin the old road now leading to the left and your parked vehicle.

42. LITTLE MOUNTAIN

Vies with few other spots on Vancouver Island for providing the most easily accessible, dizzyingly airy views. The beautiful foreground of rounded, mossy, rock surfaces, windblown firs, manzanita bushes and arbutus are the considerable cream on a great cake.

LOCATION

From Highway 19, near Parksville, turn onto Highway 4 towards Port Alberni. About 900 m along, turn left onto Bellevue Road. Drive just under 500 m and turn left onto Little Mountain Road. Drive to the end of the road, a little over 1 km along. Park against one of the concrete barriers in the small parking area. There are lots of chain-link fences and utility buildings/transmission towers.

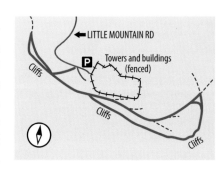

DISTANCE

1.2 km

ELEVATION GAIN

70 m

DIFFICULTY

Most paths are clear and smooth, though a few spots are a little slippery when wet, particularly along trails where moss covers smooth rock. Most of the rock surfaces are conglomerate, however, and therefore provide good traction. Children – and everyone else – should stay well back from the unfenced cliff edges.

SEASON

All season, but clear weather is best for views. Morning light is best for photographing the snow-clad mountains, since they are backlit in the afternoon.

OF SPECIAL INTEREST FOR CHILDREN

The dizzying sense of height and the likelihood of spotting eagles or (in summer) vultures soaring on the updrafts *below* should thrill most children.

1. From the parking area, walk a short distance back down the road until you come to a break in the concrete barriers and a metal gate. A clear path runs around the end of the gate. Ignore the service road heading uphill on your left. March straight out towards a cliff-edge viewpoint. Hold onto your hats and prepare to gasp.

2. Though this isn't the best viewpoint, it's still more or less stunning – particularly if Mt. Arrowsmith to the right and Mt. Moriarty (left) are sporting snow. Turn left and head up the slope, past all the utility structures, for an even better viewpoint. Turn away from cliff edge a little past the last fenced-in area and turn onto a clear, broad path running parallel to the cliff but well back. Reserve the cliff-edge route for the return leg of the loop, since walking generally uphill is a little more secure. Once along this trail, ignore the fork to the left and, a little farther along, a second, much smaller fork (there is a little gravel at the beginning of this trail).

3. Gradually descending through small firs and arbutus, come to another fork, with a well-used trail leading off to your right and downhill. Don't take this trail, but, instead, turn left to find yourself along the crest of a mossy ridge, with glimpses on the left and below of the lumps and bumps of a technical mountain-biking trail, running through the salal and small firs.

FROM LEFT Mt. Arrowsmith from the sheer cliffs of Little Mountain; the view southwest from the exposed conglomerate rock promontory at the summit.

4. Dropping down off the end of the mossy ridge, take the left fork onto a comparatively narrow trail, marked with three crosses in red spray paint on three firs.

5. This narrow trail, largely through salal, leads gradually downhill towards the end of the whole Little Mountain ridge. As you approach the end of this trail, note a trail branching to the right. This short trail is a shortcut to the second phase of your loop walk. If you have small or hyper and clumsy children with you, take this shortcut! Otherwise, go straight ahead to a kind of crossroads, at this writing marked with green and orange ribbons. Some intrepid souls take the steep trail straight ahead to drop off the end of the mountain. You, however, have saved the best view spots for now. Turn right and begin to climb along the cliff-edge trail, being a little careful at one narrow section to marshal scampering children.

6. On the first, southeast-facing section of the trail, keep your eyes peeled for a gap in the trees that allows you a magical view of three islands in the distance – Mistaken Island and the two Ballenas Islands. You soon come to your first significant viewpoint as the trail curves right. From here you can see Notch Hill and a small slice of Nanoose Bay. To the right

of a series of humps, pick out the distinctively pyramidal Mt. Benson.

7. The walk along the cliff-edge trail back towards the transmission towers is splendid. If you brought your camera you will take a long time to go a short distance. At various points you can get great angles along the jutting overhangs of the broken edge of the cliff. If, at any point, you feel uncomfortably close to the edge, there are many routes you can take well away from the edge, and some of them even behind vegetation.

8. Returning to the highest and most open viewpoint near the transmission towers, and pausing long enough to savour the sense of exhilaration, begin the second descending loop in the opposite direction. This less-popular route is well worth making. Not only do you get some splendid angles on the ragged edge of the cliff but you descend a little into the tops of some beautiful, large Douglas firs rising from the bottom of the cliff below you.

9. The trails away from the cliff edge here aren't always distinct. Clear enough under trees, they become vague when crossing open, mossy rock. However, since all are within a short distance of the cliff-edge trail, you can simply pick the most comfortable route both down this slope and back up. At one point it was possible to descend much farther than it is now: property owners have pushed out the corner of their chain-link fence onto a steep mossy bluff, making farther progress dangerous. Probably the best turnaround spot is on a mossy opening scarred by a fire pit. It is possible to go a little farther to an interesting woodpecker tree with an equally interesting double trunk, but the trail gets increasingly dotted with potentially dangerous spots.

10. Return to your vehicle by re-ascending the slope, choosing the route through the threading, small paths to suit your comfort level.

43. ENGLISHMAN RIVER ESTUARY

An easy, level stroll through huge cottonwoods by the gravel bars and banks of the Englishman River, leading to views across the sea meadows, mainland mountains and Mt. Arrowsmith.

LOCATION
From Highway 19A, in Parksville, two blocks west of the orange bridge over the Englishman River, turn in the direction of the sea onto Shelly Road, and drive the four blocks to the end of the road. Park in the clearly designated parking area by the yellow barriers.

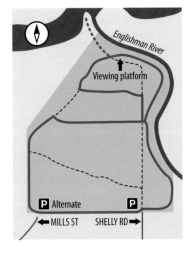

DISTANCE
2.5 km

ELEVATION GAIN
Negligible

DIFFICULTY
Easy

SEASON
All season. Even in a dry summer this part of the river has some deep pools. Much of this part of the river is tidal so will change character considerably at high tide. Fall is good for spawning salmon, but they are not always easy to spot. Come in May to June for an amazing, bowerlike walk through banks of wild roses.

OF SPECIAL INTEREST FOR CHILDREN
This is one of the few trails in the area where children can ride their bicycles while their parents walk. There are a few good spots for picnicking or splashing in the river, but the best spots require you to walk a little upstream from the trails. A raised viewing platform

is fun to climb – especially, of course, if winged beasts are about. (You shouldn't see many Canada geese amongst them because the expanding numbers and their ravenous appetites for estuary vegetation were causing damage, many were culled in 2016.) Perhaps most appealing for the younger set is a series of wee beasties (toybox escapees) that have been known to poke their noses out of various nooks along the riverside section of the trail.

You can shorten the route noted below by simply walking in a large square, without twice cutting across the central forest section.

---

1. Pass the blue metal gate, turn right and follow the dirt trail around the end of a broken-down fence barrier to make your way directly to the shore of the river under a bower of maples and alders.

2. When you reach the banks of the river, directly opposite a large island/gravel bar, turn left to follow the mainly riverside trail downstream. The view across the river is convincingly forested, providing an attractive screen between the river and Plummer Road. As you walk through the overarching grand firs, cedars, cottonwoods and Douglas firs, notice some of the more interesting trees, starting off with a dense cluster of five large maples. Two or three minutes later, look on your left where several cedars with suspended roots have apparently sprouted out of a single nurse log, now nearly rotted away.

3. As you reach the end of the first section the path turns away from the main flow of the river to run along small channels, all winding towards the distant river mouth. Dotting the sea meadows are the silver-bleached hulks of large stumps and logs that have been washed down the river during winter floods. The end of this section of the path is marked by a bench, a cairn and an inviting viewing platform. Now is the time to whip out your binoculars.

FROM LEFT The tidal flats of the estuary at low tide near the viewing platform; the view towards distant Parksville and Mt. Arrowsmith.

4. At the nearby fork in the trail, you will probably want to make an out-and-back wander along the waterside trail (to the right), though you won't be tempted to go close to the unlovely trailer park you see in the distance. Returning to this junction, turn back away from the river mouth. Even here you pass some beautifully winding river channels and, on a clear day, mouth-watering views of Mt. Arrowsmith.

5. This section of the trail has a completely different character from the riverside part as you walk through wild rose bushes and crabapple trees, past meadows dotted with character firs. At the first major branch, turn left to enter the forest again. Walk under the large trees until you come to a T junction near the main river. Turn right, walk a short distance to the first significant branch to your right and turn right to follow the trail back to the open meadows.

6. Again, turn left and follow the perimeter. Cross a small bridge and turn left when you come to a second trailhead for the park. The broad path back to your car is more functional than attractive, unless you like looking at the backs of houses.

44. BONNELL CREEK FALLS

A sequence of four falls, in winter and spring impressive both for their size and their setting within a deep, forested gorge. Although this is a very popular spot with locals, it is not in a park, so the trails are not maintained, and signs may be posted forbidding entry. It is best to check with Island Timberlands before setting out.

LOCATION

Using the Petro-Canada station in Nanoose Bay as your landmark, turn up Summerset Road, 500 m south. After 300 m, keep straight ahead on Sea Blush Drive for 500 m, and then turn right onto Sun Dew Place. In less than 100 m, stop at a red metal gate and a logging road beyond. Park on the shoulder.

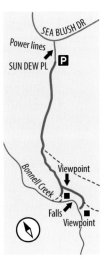

DISTANCE
2.2 km

ELEVATION GAIN
50 m, cumulative

DIFFICULTY

The approach road and trail are easy, but a few spots on the trail can be a little bushy and steep. Venturing beyond the comfortable viewpoint can be dangerous, especially in muddy conditions. Small, dodgy paths are worn to precipitous viewpoints below the falls. Above the falls a steep descent on a rooty bank has been somewhat improved by the presence of a sturdy rope. However, even this route can be dangerous.

SEASON

All season, but the falls can shrink to a trickle at the end of a dry summer. Best when the leaves are off the trees to allow the clearest view from the top of the bank.

OF SPECIAL INTEREST FOR CHILDREN

When full, the series of falls, with its thundering rush and spray filling the air, is thrilling. However, only older children and those who will obey their Sensible Parents should be brought to this spectacular spot.

1. Pass by the red gate, cross under the power lines and walk straight ahead on the major gravel road leading through an open gravel area. After 400 m, partway around the curve in the road to the left, turn onto a clear broad track (looking roughly like a Jeep track) leading down to the right through the recently logged area.

2. This track gradually heads towards the stream and a stand of large trees along the edges of the gorge. Soon you are in earshot of the roar from the falls, amplified by the steep, rocky sides of a deep ravine. A much-used trail on the right leads down to a series of viewpoints of the entire set of several falls. This small trail goes farther but becomes increasingly dangerous and does not afford better views.

3. Return the short distance to the junction and turn right to follow the trail upstream, roughly parallel to the gorge. At one point, the trail is narrow and steep, requiring some care. The trail soon broadens as you pass a large fir marked with red paint and, shortly after, a second, paint-marked tree.

4. Turn right down a small trail towards Bonnell Creek, now above the falls. From a safe vantage point, catch glimpses of the churning pools above the falls. The rest of the trail is mostly used by locals who make the steep and possibly dangerous, rope-assisted descent towards the creek. The deep pool at the base of the trail is particularly popular with daredevil divers. Fawn lilies dot the lower slopes in April.

5. Retrace your steps along the gravel road back to your vehicle.

CLOCKWISE FROM ABOVE LEFT Three of the four falls from the lower viewpoint; the double falls is second from the top; the lower falls seem to carry the most force; winter floods transform the falls.

45. ENOS LAKE & THE LAKES DISTRICT

Immensely varied route including one trail along a small stream under large cedars and another across open, mossy bluffs with views along a lovely lake.

LOCATION

On Highway 19, midway between Nanaimo and Parksville, look for the Nanoose Bay Petro-Canada station at a set of traffic lights. Turn onto Northwest Bay Road and proceed for 1.2 km, then go right onto Powder Point Road. After 2.5 km, look for a gravel parking area on your left backed by a low, split-cedar fence.

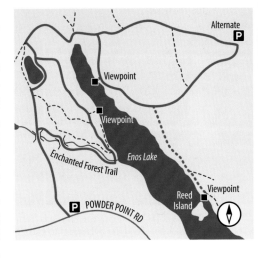

At present, a professional-looking trail map is displayed here, but beware, the map is disturbingly misleading!

DISTANCE

4.5 km, mostly loops

ELEVATION GAIN

85 m, cumulative, over generally rolling terrain

DIFFICULTY

Easy, safe trails, though some areas can be muddy – very muddy – and in a few places, roots or rocks can be slippery.

SEASON

All season. The "enchanted" route along a stream to the "Fairy Glen" waterfall dries out during most summers.

OF SPECIAL INTEREST FOR CHILDREN

The trail passes next to a giant anthill, in summer seething with little critters. The idyllic pond is full of frogs, ducks, water lilies, dragon flies and cattails, and the mossy bluffs overlooking Enos Lake scream "Picnic!" The real highlight for most children might be the Enchanted Forest Trail where, peering out from various mossy nooks, are tiny toy creatures, monsters and action figures – unless they have wandered off by the time you arrive.

The route described here is one of many possible within a complex network of trails. The good news is that this network is slated to be expanded and organized into a large regional park. The bad news is that the current expanse of forest and bluffs, as part of the same plan, is also slated to be encroached upon by pockets of housing development. Visit as soon as possible to enjoy it at its best.

---

1. The first part of the route follows a broad, much-travelled track, descending, past a huge anthill, through scattered trees, mostly Douglas firs.

2. Cross a simple bridge. Note the trail on your left since your return is along that trail. Turn right to follow a small stream overshadowed by cedars: this is the time to begin the quest for wee creatures tucked into the foliage. Because the ground is bare in one area, the trail is indistinct, but once you have crossed a little bridge to the right bank of the little stream, keep on that side until you drop fairly steeply to Enos Lake. As you cross the stream for the third time, look upstream to be charmed by an elegant little waterfall in a fern-lined cleft.

3. From the lakeshore, the trail almost immediately begins to climb. (There is a small trail running along the edge of the lake itself, but it becomes rough.) As the trail climbs to mossy bluffs you begin a sequence of great lake views. At a fork, keep right to descend fairly steeply through a grove of firs, before rising again to follow a long section of exposed,

CLOCKWISE FROM TOP LEFT The view of Enos Lake from the bluffs; the miniature falls in the "Fairy Glen" near the end of the Enchanted Forest Trail; the small duck and waterlily pond.

mossy bluffs dotted with arbutus. Ignore two trails leading to the left over rocky knolls.

4. At a T junction by the pond, turn right to reach another T junction with a broad cross trail and a posted map. Turn right to descend a gravelly road to the head of Enos Lake. While this end of the lake has been disrupted by a kind of broken boulder dam (the lake once was used as a water supply), the view down the lake itself is lovely.

5. Once past the end of the lake, turn right to join a level, dirt path first under small lodgepole pines and firs. Follow this path along and slightly above the shore of the lake until you come to a viewpoint on your right, inviting you to leave the trail and pause, possibly even to dabble your toes in the lake. Returning to the trail, climb gradually away from the lake along the broad trail. At a fork in the trail, where the main trail swings left and uphill, you may wish to explore down

the smaller right fork before returning to this point. If you do explore this route, you should know that it runs along the lake parallel to the lakeshore, leading to a viewpoint onto an unusual little island of reeds. Arthurian myths may just spring to mind! Just before this view spot, note a significant trail angling off uphill through a corridor of small firs. This leads to some lovely, mossy bluffs with views over the straits.

Beware: the network of trails up there can be confusing. Likewise, a small trail continues along the lakeshore for a short distance before heading uphill. This, too, leads to a lovely web of small trails but is too rough to be recommended.

---

6. Retrace the trail back to the posted map. At this junction with the map, turn away from the lake, rising considerably and passing areas of sword fern and mossy bluffs. At the high point, pass a small trail on your left. When you descend and come to a T junction, note a parking area. Turn left away from this parking area to follow an old road back to the head of the lake. Retrace your route past the lake, climbing up the gravel road and passing on the left the trail that brought you to the gravel road.

7. This broad track curves around to your left, bringing you to a junction with a smaller trail leading off to the left. Again, turn left to retrace this trail, too, along the shore of the pond, now on your right. This time keep straight ahead, following the shore of the pond. Although the trail can be rough at spots, and the bordering salal a little too lush, this is the place to spot ducks, water lilies, frogs, cattails and dragonflies.

8. Reach the main trail at a T junction again and turn left. Follow this large track, until you come to the bridge and the beginning of the Enchanted Forest Trail. From here, follow your outbound route back to your vehicle, trying not to be dismayed at how much steeper the trail now seems.

46. NOTCH HILL

A loop through varied vegetation, in some areas a deep forest of Douglas firs and ferns, and in others meadows of Garry oaks and arbutus. Magnificently airy views down Nanoose Bay towards Nanaimo and east over Nanoose Bay towards Mt. Moriarty and Mt. Arrowsmith. Currently private property open to visitors, but, according to plans, in the process of becoming a regional park.

LOCATION

On Highway 19, midway between Nanaimo and Parksville, look for the Nanoose Bay Petro-Canada station at a set of traffic lights. Turn onto Northwest Bay Road and proceed for 1.2 km, then 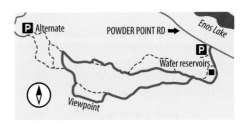 go right onto Powder Point Road. After 3.4 km, you see a gravel parking area up a slope to your right and a sign reading "Fairwinds Notch Hill."

DISTANCE

2.1 km, mostly loop

ELEVATION GAIN

180 m, cumulative

DIFFICULTY

Easy and clear trail, but perhaps a bit epic for small children. A few rough spots over solid rock, but nothing precipitous.

SEASON

All year, but views of the mountains are best in clear weather, when the mountains are under snow, usually mid-November to mid-summer.

OF SPECIAL INTEREST FOR CHILDREN

The exposed rock near the top with its bumps and lumps encourages safe climbing and jumping. Any of the three good view spots is perfect for a picnic. The huge hulk of a woodpecker tree can be fun to spot.

1. From the parking area start up a gravel service road, passing a broad, level path at the edge of the parking area. A map of the whole area has been thoughtfully posted near this junction, but currently the map is inaccurate. (Locals have printed and posted more accurate, plastic-covered maps at various points throughout the trails.)

2. Pass a metal gate and ignore a broad track to the right leading to two large water reservoirs. Ascend through some firs and enter a small open meadow area dotted with Garry oaks and posted with a colourful and informative sign. Ignore a trail leading to the left (this will be your return route).

3. Enter the trees and, after a short distance, ignore a broad smooth trail on your right. (This is a less-attractive loop trail, rejoining the main route a short distance ahead.)

4. Emerge from the trees to a more open area of arbutus and Garry oaks, climbing towards the summit. Pick your way over a few spots of solid rock where you need to choose your route just before the summit area. The entire top of the hill is quite large, with various lumps and bumps of moss-covered basalt. The best views towards Nanaimo are from the first area you come to, but, for the best views of Mt. Arrowsmith, continue along the trail through a small area of firs to another open crest. There is a choice of routes here, but they converge as the trail begins to descend.

5. Begin the descent over some fairly steep, but not precipitous, sections of rock. As you enter the trees and continue your descent, look out for a narrow but clear trail to your left, traversing a slope horizontally.

CLOCKWISE FROM LEFT Arbutus dot the bluffs overlooking the end of Nanoose Bay; the view looking south towards distant Nanaimo; in winter snow, the hill remains a deservedly popular family walk.

6. Turn left here and drop to join a broad roadbed. Turn left along this roadbed. At this point you are in the notch that gives the double-crested hill its name. After a short time enjoying the sense of being in an unusual bit of geography, deep in a forest, you come to a smaller, but well-trod, path to your right, leading upward.

7. Turn right and wind up through the thinning trees until they open out to reveal an exposed rock bluff with more excellent views down and across Nanoose Bay. Follow the trail to the left, dropping gradually and re-entering the trees to rejoin the trail you left earlier. In winter you may have to use a little light-footed scrambling to cross a small, wet area.

8. Turn right to follow the broad track, watching out for a woodpecker tree on your left – a large Douglas fir full of holes. Reconnect with your outbound trail in the oak meadow. Either return to your vehicle the way you came or take the short alternate route past the reservoirs.

47. KNARSTON CREEK

*A winding forest trail largely running parallel
to a small rushing creek surrounded by sword ferns
and large, old firs, cedars and hemlocks.*

This route is largely through the most popular part of a much larger trail system called Copley Ridge Trails (the registered, signposted trails are mostly old logging roads, but many other trails used criss-cross the slopes of the ridge). The people of Lantzville deserve enormous credit for establishing and maintaining the trails and bridges in this BC forest woodlot.

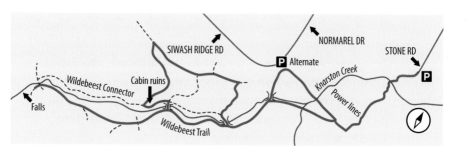

LOCATION
At the traffic lights by the prominent Lantzville Firehall, 3 km north of Woodgrove Shopping Centre, turn away from the ocean onto Superior Road. Follow Superior Road uphill as it curves to the right, for about 0.6 km. Turn left onto Stone Road and follow it 0.5 km to its end. Given the popularity of the trail, usually there are several cars on either side of the broad shoulder and the wide entrance to the trail immediately to the left of a driveway.

DISTANCE
4.1 km, mostly loop, with many longer options

ELEVATION GAIN
80 m

DIFFICULTY

Easy to moderate, requiring a little care on some rooty sections. Some of the adjoining routes involve more considerable ascents.

SEASON

All season, though, unsurprisingly, the path can be soggy and slippery in wet conditions. Knarston Creek – and its two sets of waterfalls – flow most prettily during the wet season. Some of the alternate trails require crossing the creek over stepping stones, obviously easier when the creek is low or dry.

OF SPECIAL INTEREST FOR CHILDREN

As long as the fast-flowing creek is full of water, the appeal of stick-boat races and other watery mayhem is obvious. The trail itself, twisting and rising over knolls and through big trees, has something of that "enchanted forest" atmosphere that can stir the imagination in some lively children. Colourful, illustrated signs provide information and can stimulate quests – starting with the dull Oregon grape and moving onto the pileated wood-pecker! The burnt-out ruins of a cabin, too, might be the source of a bit of imaginative storytelling.

1. Immediately upon entering the broad, evenly graded trail under cedars, pass signs. Pause to look at the overview map of the main Copley Ridge Trails, but be aware that many of the trails (including many on this suggested route) do not appear on this map. Descend along the snaking trail, making your way down the potentially muddiest bit of this whole route, and come to a rustic, split-log bridge. This, the first of several bridges you cross, is also the smallest and least engineered. Beyond the bridge, the trail climbs gradually through the forest towards the increasingly visible power lines.

2. Turn right along the signposted route (Copley Ridge Trail) and carry on straight ahead to follow the power lines to a paved road and an alternate trailhead. From the shoulder of the road, turn a sharp left to follow another encouragingly

FROM LEFT The upper falls tumble down a deep cleft at the end of the recommended walk; the lower falls are best viewed by leaving the path and climbing a little down the slope.

broad and signposted trail into the forest. Soon you will cross an impressively sturdy, railed bridge (again over Knarston Creek) and pass a hand-carved sign announcing the beginning of Knarston Creek Loop. Within minutes, pass an interpretative sign and reach a fork. Ignore the trail to the left (with one of the green Copley Ridge Trail signs), though note it for your return route. For now, carry on upstream, with the creek gurgling busily on your right.

3. A few minutes later, when you reach a fork, turn right to descend towards the small bridge over the creek. Now on the north side of Knarston Creek, notice a split in the trail, with one branch to your left and another slightly right and uphill, both signposted. It is possible to shorten the suggested route here and follow the trail upstream to another bridge and rejoin the suggested route. For the longer, suggested route, go slightly right to ascend through a salal-lined, winding trail.

4. When you reach a T junction with a broad roadbed, turn left to follow the signposted route gradually uphill. Keep straight ahead past a broad trail on your right. A little farther on, again keep straight ahead on the signposted route past another track on your left. You may pass a rakishly leaning phone booth (unless the prankster has relented and removed it) before you come to the next clearing, and a leafy trail leading slightly uphill on your left.

5. Although the sign encourages you to go straight ahead on the roadbed, turn left to begin your descent on this salal-lined trail. Winding prettily down a kind of ridge, the trail crosses one potentially wet spot, and, after a minute or two, brings you to a junction near the creek. Notice the hand-carved sign saying "Cabin Connector" and, nearby, another sign saying "Wildebeest Connector." It is possible to turn upstream to follow the fairly rough Wildebeest Connector and join the recommended route, but doing so will require you to cross the stream on stepping stones. Much easier (and more interesting) is the route to the left, downstream. In a very short distance, come to the burnt-out ruins of a cabin, and, just afterwards, a magnificent Douglas fir with a "Wildlife Tree" sign, and more colourfully, a hand-carved sign saying "Big Beauti [sic]" – as, indeed, it is!

6. Winding a little away from the stream and passing a golf ball (really!) nailed to a fir, the trail soon approaches the stream again to lead to another small bridge. Cross the bridge and ascend to a T junction. Turn right (though notice that you must return to this spot after you visit the upper falls). The trail climbs slowly away from the creek, soon bringing you to a fascinating Douglas fir "wolf tree," that is, the kind of multi-crowned or deformed large tree whose unique shape protects it from loggers who just can't be bothered! No wonder the tree has been called "The Beast" – at least, according to a hand-carved sign placed on its trunk.

FROM LEFT A shaft of sunlight catches one of many large cedars leaning over the stream; the creek rushes through a narrow cleft in the rock near a sharp bend.

7. The trail stays fairly high above and away from the creek for some distance. Keep straight ahead, ignoring first a cross trail and then two trails angling in from the left. Descending again to the streambed, pass a sign for Wildebeest Connector – you can safely assume more imagination than biology was involved in the naming of the trail. A trail drops to cross the stream on your right: this is where you would arrive if you had taken Wildebeest Connector earlier. Keep ahead and climb slightly to arrive at your destination and turnaround spot, a pretty set of cascading falls overhung with ferns and criss-crossed with fallen trees.

8. Return the way you came until you come to the T junction where you last crossed the creek (though you can't quite see the bridge from this junction). Keep ahead on this side of the creek. The trail swings away from the stream for some distance before turning back near the lower bridge you crossed to follow the signposted route on your outward journey. Keep ahead on this side of the creek. Just below this bridge, leave the trail, camera in hand, to find a spot in the low brush to view the little waterfalls. Regaining the path, return the

way you came along the signposted route until you come to the fork with signs pointing both straight ahead and to the right. You may recognize the trail straight ahead as part of your outbound route. This time, turn right. After a few minutes you must cross a small tributary of Knarston Creek, possibly making use of the planks provided.

9. Leaving the forest to enter the cleared strip under the power lines, come to a signposted T junction. Turn right to follow your outbound route into the forest, and crossing the split-log bridge, climb slightly back to your vehicle. Congratulate yourself for having made your way through one of the more labyrinthine routes in this book!

Optional Add-On: Beginning at Stone Road

If you are interested in a long walk on these trails and don't mind skirting the prettiest trail (described here), choose the most easily followed, well-signposted loop beginning (like the shorter route described above) at Stone Road.

1. Stone Road leaves Superior Road shortly before Normarel Drive. From the end of Stone Road, follow the signs to the power lines. Turn left under the power lines until you see the sign pointing uphill under trees. Climb until you reach an abandoned logging road.

2. Turn right at the sign to follow roadbeds for several kilometres, climbing significantly and passing two view spots. Walk down a steep section and come to a signposted T junction.

3. Leave the main roadbed to turn right and begin your gradual descent towards the power lines. At one point you see a sign directing you to make a sharp right turn. Cross Knarston Creek and join the creekside trail described in the main trip, until you come to the power lines. Turn right to rejoin your outward path near Stone Road.

48. AMMONITE FALLS REGIONAL TRAIL

Perhaps the loveliest falls on Vancouver Island, Ammonite Falls (in Benson Creek Falls Regional Park) drops without impediment as a single sheet of water, framed by the curving strata of shale and large firs.

LOCATION

From the Nanaimo Parkway (Highway 19), turn onto Jingle Pot Road at the traffic lights opposite Mostar Road. (Jingle Pot Road crosses the parkway twice – this is the northwest exit, near Woodgrove Shopping Centre.) Drive along Jingle Pot Road for 4.6 km and turn right onto Kilpatrick Road. After 800 m, turn right onto Jameson Road and continue for just under 2.5 km, until you see Creekside Place on your right. Turn downhill onto Creekside Place and, after 200 m, turn into the large gravel parking area for Benson Creek Falls Regional Park. Do not attempt to park on any approach roads to the trailhead – your familymobile will be towed!

Benson Creek Falls Regional Park can also be approached from its other side, via Doumont Road, but there is no easily passable connection between the north side of the river gorge and this, its south side – though it is tantalizing to think of a suspension bridge connecting the two.

DISTANCE

4.8-km return (plus optional extension)

ELEVATION GAIN

220 m, cumulative

DIFFICULTY

The trail to the falls is fairly easy, though a little rooty in sections. Expect to puff on the return leg. The trail at the falls to the fenced viewing area, though short, is quite steep and awkward. The trail to the base of the falls, in spite of its rope, is very steep and cannot be recommended.

SEASON

The falls can dry to a trickle at the end of a dry summer. Late fall through early summer is therefore usually best for those magic moments.

OF SPECIAL INTEREST FOR CHILDREN

The view of the deep canyon overhung with large trees and the falls themselves, plunging out of sight, should thrill even the most battlestar-jaded child.

1. Walk from the parking lot uphill along Creekside Place to its junction with Jameson Road and turn right along the gravel road towards a yellow metal gate. You should see one of the small, blue-and-white regional trail signs that henceforth helps you on your way to the falls. Pass the gate for a long tromp uphill along this forestry research road.

2. Ignore a gravel road angling off to the left. Turn right onto a signposted smaller track leading downhill through the salal. Ignore a small trail leading off to your left. Drop into a little dip, cross a small wooden bridge and climb a short distance up onto a ridge. The trail runs a little way through smaller trees and drops down a short, steep slope.

3. Ignore the right fork in the trail, turning sharp left to follow the signpost. Look for lovely little deer ferns along this trail – very unusual for the east coast of Vancouver Island. When you emerge onto a gravel road, look across and a little to the left and see the signposted continuation of the trail, soon curving to the left towards more solid forest.

CLOCKWISE FROM LEFT The sheer drop of the falls down shale cliffs makes for a particularly lovely scene; the falls from the official viewpoint at the top of the falls; the falls of Flynfall Creek can be seen only by walking along this optional extra trail.

4. After a few minutes, arrive at a T junction with a well-used trail. Turn right, as the signpost indicates. In a minute or two, you come to an unsignposted split in the trail. Worry not: both trails rise and drop over a small ridge, rejoining at the bottom. When you see the sign for Benson Creek Falls Regional Park, you know you're near your destination.

5. Arriving at a cleared area under several small cedars, make your way to many spots where you can look down into the deep gorge. You can see Benson Creek approaching from the left around an exceptionally sharp curve then dropping away to the top of the falls on the right. To get a better view of the falls themselves, you must make your way down a fairly steep dirt track on the downstream end of this open area. Roots and an improvised rope will help, though the trail isn't dangerous. A chain-link fence is on your left, which allows you some good views of the top of the falls, plunging almost vertically under your feet.

6. If you want to see Flynfall Creek Falls, skip ahead to the Optional Add-On below. If you want to return to your vehicle, take the much-used downward path to the bottom of the falls, which is considerably steeper than your upward journey, though supplied with marginally trustworthy ropes. A yellow sign warns you not to "proceed beyond this point."

7. Return the way you came or continue.

Optional Add-On: Flynfall Creek Falls

1. From the clearing above the viewing spot, look for a broad, smooth trail heading downstream. Turn left onto this trail and follow it through salal and small firs. Notice the small orange plastic diamonds along the trail.

2. When, after a few minutes, you see a smaller, newly cut and somewhat rough trail on your left, notice that the orange markers are dotted down this trail. Turn onto this trail. It soon smooths out and arrives at a T junction with a larger trail. Turn left to follow this broad trail as it leads towards an increasingly narrow ridge formed by a sharp bend in Benson Creek.

3. As you approach the narrowest end of the ridge – and if you arrive during wet season – look to your left and see the lovely, showering falls created by Flynfall Creek dropping into Benson Creek. The trail continues straight ahead, soon turning into a steep, dirt track switchbacking down off the end of the ridge. Before bothering with this trail, consider that it arrives at the bank of the creek where the only forward way is via a difficult, mossy tree trunk that forms a rough bridge (to the other part of the park).

4. It is best, therefore, to linger a little at the viewpoint at the top of the ridge and retrace your route past Ammonite Falls to your vehicle.

49. LINLEY VALLEY & COTTLE LAKE

*An amazingly hidden valley and lake in an upland area
in the north end of Nanaimo, Linley Valley Cottle Lake Park
is one of those "Who wudda thunk?!" places.*

LOCATION
From Highway 19 in north
Nanaimo, near the Country
Club Shopping Centre, turn
at the traffic lights north onto
Norwell Drive. After 250 m,
turn right onto Departure Bay
Road and drive for 750 m. Make
a left turn onto Rock City Road
and drive about 1.3 km, until
you see a small parking area on
your left and a large, colourful
map and sign.

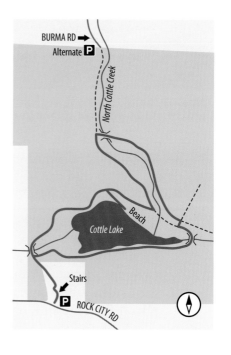

DISTANCE
2.2-km loop

ELEVATION GAIN
90 m, cumulative

DIFFICULTY
Mostly easy, smooth trails, but the section on the south shore of
the lake is very rooty and uneven.

SEASON
All season

OF SPECIAL INTEREST FOR CHILDREN
A lake? A swimming beach? Ducks aplenty? Few items rank
higher on most children's list of magnets.

FROM LEFT The hidden valley viewed from the bench near the beginning of the trail; the east end of the lake narrows into a rich tangle of growth.

Beware: the large, colourful and meticulously produced map you see posted at more than one trailhead, and online, bares fascinatingly tenuous connection with reality. The signposts, too, can be puzzling.

---

1. Note the signpost pointing to Burma Road (a trailhead at the north border of the park) and descend the magnificently twisting, suspended wooden staircase down, down into the hidden valley. Emerging from the trees into a kind of plateau meadow area, carry on along the main path over a storybook stone bridge (no, you are not in Europe, despite appearances). Pause when you come to a park bench with its lovely (no other word will do) views over the winding paths of the meadow and towards the west end of Cottle Lake.

2. Dropping down to lake level, follow the (slightly overgrown) crushed-gravel path along the west edge of the meadow. Swing to your right at the signpost for Lake Trail. Pass over a boardwalk through marsh grass and begin the heavily forested (and rough) trail along the south shore of this little lake. Although the species of ducks may vary seasonally, the number seems not to. Have your binoculars and camera ready.

3. Reaching the end of the lake, follow the trail to the left over a prettily curving and solid bridge. Climb a few concrete steps and pass three interesting Douglas firs, more or less joined at the base. Ignore a trail to the left and pass a sign for Lake Trail pointing back the way you came. Almost immediately afterward, come to an unsignposted crossroads and turn left.

4. Your new trail leads gradually uphill, soon running parallel to North Cottle Creek (looking in summer like little more than a low bushy strip to your left). After crossing a bridge, come almost immediately to a broad, road-width trail. Notice a sign pointing, variously, to "Burma," "Linley" and "Binkerton Bluff." Turn left to descend gradually, now on the other side of North Cottle Creek. Ignore an unmapped dirt trail leading off to your right.

5. When you arrive at another bridge, you should see a very confusing sign, pointing, variously, to "Lake Trail," "Burma" (in the direction from which you have come) and "Linley." If you fail to make much sense of the sign, worry not. Simply turn right immediately before the bridge.

6. Walk the short distance to an unsignposted junction with a broad dirt trail leading downhill towards the lake. Although this trail is a dead end (except for a very rough and overgrown trail leading to the east end of the lake), it is worth making the short walk to the lake. After all, this, one of two easy access spots for the lakeshore, is probably the nicer.

7. After splashing, eating or simply appreciating this pretty bit of shore viewing, return the short distance uphill to the junction and turn left. The trail curves back towards the shore of the lake and the second beach. Leaving the beach behind you, walk through the meadows at the end of the lake, very soon passing outhouses and a picnic table. From here it is only a short distance, over two small bridges, back to the junction for Lake Trail, and, of course, your climb back to your vehicle.

View across the lake from the north shore

USEFUL CONTACTS

BC Parks » gov.bc.ca/bcparks

Capital Regional District Parks » crd.bc.ca/parks
Tel: 250.478.3344 Fax: 250.478.5416

Comox Valley Regional District Parks and Trails
» comoxvalleyrd.ca/parks-recreation/parks-trails
Tel: 250.334.6000 Toll free: 1.800.331.6007

Cowichan Valley Regional District » cvrd.bc.ca
Tel: 250.746.2500 Toll free: 1.800.665.3955

Fisheries & Oceans Canada » dfo-mpo.gc.ca
Tides and shellfish closures: 250.339.2031
Communications Branch Tel: 604.666.0384 Fax: 604.666.1847

Horne Lake Caves Provincial Park » hornelake.com
For information on how to prepare for a self-guided visit:
env.gov.bc.ca/bcparks/explore/parkpgs/horne_lk

Island Timberlands Land » blog.islandtimberlands.cwom
Before using trails, check the company's blog site for the most
recent advisories and closures.

Pacific Rim National Park » pc.gc.ca/pacificrim
Tel: 250.726.3500 Fax: 250.726.3520

Regional District of Nanaimo, Recreation & Parks Services
» rdn.bc.ca
Tel: 250.248.3252 Toll free within BC: 1.888.828.2069
Fax: 250.248.3159 Email: recparks@rdn.bc.ca

ACKNOWLEDGEMENTS

Thanks to Bill "Pathfinder" Thomson, Ted Wheeler, and Scott Davidson for helping with the exploration of out-of-the-way trails.